It is becoming increasingly evident that a business environment which is devoid of ethics and socially-aware decision-making is no longer sustainable. This book by Richard Higginson provides some refreshing and challenging biblical reflections on faith in business. It is a timely and much needed contribution that will help business professionals and organisations – whether local or global – to engage their consciences and re-examine their attitudes towards financial systems and financial practices with regards to ethics and morality.

Richard offers some useful material to stimulate healthy discussion and debate. The solution depends on our own personal attitudes and where we draw the line for ourselves in terms of personal wealth and business ethics. Mahatma Gandhi said: 'There is enough for every man's need, but not for every man's greed.'

Richard gives a number of examples of ethical businesses and business practices that benefit all parties including the organisations themselves and those who lead them, the shareholders, the producers and members of their supply chain, and the consumers themselves who are demanding higher degrees of business virtue than ever before.

Ram Gidoomal CBE Chairman, Traidcraft plc

I have been privileged to collaborate with Richard Higginson by inviting him to be a Visiting Lecturer in Canada, speaking at his conference in Cambridge, writing for *Faith in Business Quarterly* and using his writings in my university classes. I appreciate Richard's keen ability to understand the intersection of faith and business, his skill in teaching and his clarity in writing. From the common green of Ridley Hall to the corridors of powers around the world, Richard's perspective makes him uniquely qualified to convey how the Christian faith can be a power for good in the global economy.

Richard J. Goossen, PhD, Chairman, Entrepreneurial Leaders Organization

Hope is such a neglected virtue in the English psyche that it deserves this, a whole book to itself. I love the dramatic structuring of the book, and one of Higginson's strengths is his use of a wide range of biblical quotes and examples. The book will really help those Christians who kn⌐   ⌐ts them

T0324266

in their work, but struggle to find the right words to talk to their workmates about 'the hope that is in them'.
Dr Eve Poole, Ashridge Business School

This is the book I have been waiting for! Richard Higginson has drawn on his decades of research and experience to craft a definitive integration of faith and the marketplace. It is thoroughly biblical, so much so that one feels she or he has been taken on an invigorating Bible study from Genesis to Revelation, learning what the Bible says about work, interest, bribery and almost everything one encounters in the world of commercial enterprise. But it is, at the same time, grounded in the realities of the global marketplace, one which Higginson explores with fascinating case studies. While he gives 'air-time' to creative alternatives to the standard corporate model he offers what is most needed for the 'mainly-for-profit' businesses: hope. I would recommend this book not only to people in business but to every pastor who wishes to empower his or her members for the service in the Kingdom of God from Monday to Friday.
R. Paul Stevens, Professor Emeritus, Marketplace Theology, Regent College, Vancouver, BC

Well researched and theologically deep, Richard Higginson shows how the great themes of Scripture can be applied to the world of business. Connecting Christianity and commerce in a wide ranging discussion, this book fuels the debate about values and principles in business, and encourages us to make that connection work in practice.
Paul Valler Former Finance and Operations Director. Hewlett-Packard Ltd

FAITH, HOPE & THE GLOBAL ECONOMY

Richard Higginson

FAITH, HOPE & THE GLOBAL ECONOMY

A power for good

ivp

INTER-VARSITY PRESS
Norton Street, Nottingham NG7 3HR, England
Email: ivp@ivpbooks.com
Website: www.ivpbooks.com

First published 2012

British Library Cataloguing in Publication Data
A catalogue record for this book is available from the British Library.

ISBN: 978-1-84474-580-7

Set in Dante 12/15pt
Typeset in Great Britain by CRB Associates, Potterhanworth, Lincolnshire
Printed and bound in Great Britain by Ashford Colour Press Ltd, Gosport, Hampshire

Inter-Varsity Press publishes Christian books that are true to the Bible and that communicate the gospel, develop discipleship and strengthen the church for its mission in the world.

Inter-Varsity Press is closely linked with the Universities and Colleges Christian Fellowship, a student movement connecting Christian Unions in universities and colleges throughout Great Britain, and a member movement of the International Fellowship of Evangelical Students. Website: www.uccf.org.uk

CONTENTS

SERIES PREFACE

A time for courage

Work matters hugely.

Work is the primary activity God created us to pursue – in communion with him and in partnership with others. Indeed, one of work's main goals is to make God's world a better place for all God's creatures to flourish in – to his glory.

Yes, work matters hugely.

And to many people it brings the joys of purpose shared, relationships deepened, talents honed, character shaped, obstacles overcome, products made, people served and money earned – even amid the inevitable frustrations, failures and disagreements of working life in even the best of organizations.

Yes, work matters hugely. And the financial crisis that began in 2008 only served to reinforce that reality as many found themselves without paid employment, many more with less money and many, many more were gripped by the fear of losing their jobs. However, long before the crisis, work had been getting harder, longer, less satisfying and more draining. Work had stretched its voracious tentacles into almost every area of life, sucking out the zing and whoosh and ease from time with family, friends, hobbies and community activities. UK citizens, for example, work four hours longer per person per week than the citizens of any other EU nation. We live in Slave New World.

How do we follow Jesus faithfully and fruitfully in such conditions?

Is coping – getting through the week – the height of our ambition? Surely not. But do we have good news for the workplace? Not just a truth to proclaim but a way to follow?

Not just a way to follow but life, divine life, to infuse the quality of our work, the quality of our relationships at work, and the quality of our contribution to the culture of the organizations in which we work? In our current context, we need not only biblical insight and divine empowerment, but also courage to make tough decisions about work and life, and courage to make tough decisions at work. Furthermore, at this time of national soul-searching about our economy and the values that drive it, we need to learn not only how to be faithful servants in the work culture we find ourselves in, but also to become proactive, positive shapers of that culture.

That's what the Faith at Work series is designed to do: take on the tough issues facing workers and offer material that's fresh, either because it brings new insights to familiar topics or because the author's particular background and experience open up enlightening vistas. We've also tried to write the books so that there's something nutritious and tasty, not only for the leisurely diner, but also for the snacker snatching a quick read on a train, or in a break, or, indeed, at the end of a demanding day.

The Lord be with you as you read. And the Lord be with you as you seek to follow him faithfully and courageously in your workplace.

Mark Greene, Series Editor
London Institute for Contemporary Christianity, 2009

Volumes include:
Get a Life Paul Valler
Working It Out Ian Coffey
Working Without Wilting Jago Wynne
Working Models for Our Time Mark Greene (commissioned)
Ten at Work John Parmiter

ACKNOWLEDGMENTS

This book is the product of over twenty years of working alongside Christians in business as Director of the Faith in Business project at Ridley Hall. The hundreds of people who have attended our conferences, participated in seminars, written for our quarterly journal, exchanged views by email and invited me into their companies are too numerous to mention. But I am very grateful to all of them for their stimulus, support and fellowship in the gospel.

In recent years I have been privileged to travel widely, fulfilling speaking engagements and carrying out research across the world. So I would also like to thank the many friends in such countries as Canada, Chile, Sweden, Kenya, India and China who have offered me hospitality and enabled me to observe first-hand exciting and innovative business enterprises that have been inspired by God. It's a privilege to pass on their stories.

In the writing of this book I am particularly grateful to:

- my colleagues at Ridley Hall, who stood in for me while I took a term's study leave to write in the spring and summer of 2011
- my wife Felicity, who continues to lavish me with love, support and encouragement
- my friends James Allcock, Eve Poole and David Murray, who provided me with helpful comments on the first draft, and many other individuals who commented on shorter sections
- Sam Parkinson, editor at IVP, for his patient, detailed and painstaking work in helping bring the final text to completion.

My prayer is that God may use this book to help Christians to be a power for good in the global economy.

1. FAITH IN THE ECONOMY: A POWER FOR GOOD

The Christian faith, rightly understood, can be an enormous power for good in the global economy. It stimulates enterprise, reduces poverty, promotes integrity, encourages sustainability and fosters discipleship.

This claim strikes some as bold and bizarre. It appears to overestimate Christianity's scope of influence. We hear much today about the decline of the Christian faith, a trend that seems relentless and irreversible. If the strength of a faith is measured in terms of churchgoing statistics, that view appears to have plenty of support. In northern Europe (the UK, France, Germany, Belgium, the Netherlands, Scandinavia) only 4–8% of the population attend church on a weekly basis.[1] Secularization is proceeding apace.

Christian faith and the global economy also occupy very different categories in the minds of most people who are not practising Christians. They don't seem to have anything to do with each other. Christian faith is thought to be concerned with a spiritual realm: with personal salvation, forgiveness of sins and eternal life – and so in part it is. Economics is about the world of money and material goods. When I introduce myself as a theologian whose major area of interest is business, people look surprised.

Even for practising Christians in Western Europe, being a power for good in the global economy may not be a high priority. Many work in business, and all play an indirect role in the global economy as consumers and investors. But the effect of Christian faith on the way they work and spend seems to be marginal. It is widely accepted that the world of business operates along predetermined lines. There are economic laws – the laws of supply and demand, for instance, in determining wages and prices – which decide how things are, and the feeling is that Christians can do little to change them.

But the opening statement of this book is no mere theoretical claim. It is not the deluded fantasy of an armchair theologian. That Christianity is a power for economic good is something that I have seen time and time again – as I have met with businesspeople in the UK, travelled the world and delved into the past. This book will give many specific examples of Christians whose business activities have brought life and hope to their communities and countries.

It is when we take a historical and geographical perspective that the claim that Christian faith can be an enormous power for the good in the global economy makes much more sense. If we take a trip to other parts of the world now in the early twenty-first century, or if we venture back to Western Europe three centuries ago, things look very different.

Christianity worldwide
Estimating the number of adherents to the different world faiths is notoriously difficult. But most agree that Christianity is still the largest world's religion. Just over 2 billion of the world's 7 billion consider themselves Christians, at least when answering research surveys. Even allowing for many who are not *practising* Christians (they do not attend church, their beliefs are vague and their behaviour is not recognisably Christian), this volume of professed allegiance should be taken seriously. Christianity is a decidedly global faith. There are lively Christian communities in virtually every country of the world, including Islamic countries where they are persecuted or conversion to Christianity is illegal. The secularized nature of Western Europe is at odds with trends in every other

continent – 36% of Americans, 48% of Brazilians and 78% of sub-Saharan Africans attend a church service once a week.[2] Christian faith is keenly embraced in many of the countries that received it through colonization by the European civilization that has now largely abandoned it.

Globally, then, Christianity is still a force to be reckoned with. But one cannot automatically assume that, where Christians are in the ascendant, they play a positive role economically. In some countries churches have failed, by and large, to make fruitful connections between faith and business. Hence the reason for choosing words carefully in my opening sentence. I said that the Christian faith, *rightly understood*, can be an enormous power for good in the global economy. Much hangs on those words 'rightly understood'. The positive connection between faith and business does not always follow.

While the proportion of the world's population who are officially Christian is roughly the same today as it was 100 years ago (just under a third), it has changed considerably within particular countries. It has declined in Western Europe but grown in other parts of the world, notably certain Asian countries. The church in South Korea grew from virtually nothing to over 30% of the population during the second half of the twentieth century. This coincided with rapid economic growth: an annual rate of 9% between 1960 and 1990. Several commentators make a connection between the two.[3]

Attitudes of enterprise, thrift, hard work and trust, all conducive to economic growth, have been encouraged by the rise of Christianity. The same process is being repeated in contemporary China, despite the Government's ambivalent attitude to the faith. In fast-growing cities like Shanghai and Wenzhou, industrial expansion and church growth are feeding each other. There is even a new category of businessmen known as Boss Christians, so upfront are they about their allegiance and so pivotal is their faith to their way of work.[4] It is when the impact of the Christian faith on a country is new and vibrant that its power for good in the economic realm tends to be most evident.

Christianity in Europe

The positive connection between faith and business was evident in many European countries in the centuries following the Protestant Reformation. The seventeenth century was the Golden Age of the Dutch Republic. Trade, industry, art and science all flourished in a society where most skilled craftsmen and rich merchants were inspired by a lively Christian – mainly Calvinist – faith. This faith led them to respond to God's call to exercise their talents in every sphere of life. It gave the Dutch confidence and resolve in tackling their country's endemic threat of flooding. Jan Leeghwater, a pioneer of land reclamation and expert on drainage, wrote that 'the draining of the lakes is one of the most necessary, the most profitable and most holy works in Holland'.[5] Symptomatic of the enterprising, cooperative and tough-minded spirit that marked this emergent nation was the coming together of several small spice trading companies in the Dutch East India Company (VOC) in 1602. This signalled the start of a new commercial epoch. The VOC was the first joint-stock company and the sale of its shares took place on the world's first stock market.

In Britain, the Quakers were a Christian group that had an influence out of all proportion to their size. During the second half of the nineteenth century, when at the height of their commercial influence, they numbered less than 20,000 people. But the Quakers were prominent in banking, insurance, confectionery, drinks, engineering, railways, steel, soap, pharmaceuticals, shoes and textiles. Many of the great Quaker names of eighteenth- and nineteenth-century commerce, such as Lloyds, Barclays, Cadbury, Rowntree and Clarks, are still with us – some as brands under new management.

Historian James Walvin believes that the Quakers did well in business for a variety of reasons.[6] Among the factors he highlights are the following:

- The Quakers' fierce commitment to *honesty*. They were accepted as honest even by those who disliked them. During the eighteenth century this reputation made people ready to trust Quaker banks with their money. Honesty also stood them in good stead in other areas of commerce. Their word could be trusted, their goods were what they seemed, and their prices were both fixed and reasonable.
- The Quakers' system of *mutual accountability*. They kept checks on each other, and had to answer for their commercial conduct to their local meeting. Prominent Quakers met regularly, passed on business advice and warned against dubious prospects or dodgy traders. This network stretched across the Atlantic.
- The Quakers' emphasis on *education*. This flowed from the Protestant habit of reading the Bible for yourself. They set up their own schools and developed apprenticeships for their children. Sons were often sent to another Quaker associate to learn a trade before returning to run the family business.

The Protestant work ethic

All these examples of Christianity making a positive economic contribution have been Protestant. Does this mean I am reasserting the importance of the Protestant work ethic? The answer is yes – but with significant qualifications.

The phrase 'Protestant work ethic' became popular after the German sociologist Max Weber wrote *The Protestant Ethic and the Spirit of Capitalism* in 1905. Weber observed that in modern Europe – Germany in particular – the owners of capital and the higher grades of skilled labour were over-whelmingly Protestant rather than Catholic. He argued that Protestantism created the psychological conditions which facilitated the development of capitalism. It produced managers and workers who were rational, sober, industrious and thrifty. This helped their business expand, because wealth was prudently invested for future growth rather than squandered on personal vainglory. Weber described this as worldly asceticism, and saw it as especially pronounced in Calvinism.

Why should this be? Weber's explanation was that Calvin's doctrine of predestination, in which God's eternal decree divided humanity into the saved and the damned, created in people a state of lonely insecurity. Though Protestantism taught that salvation came through faith rather than works, faith could be counterfeit, so the individual was thrown back on a life of good works as a sign of God's election. Weber called good works the means 'not of purchasing salvation, but of getting rid of the fear of damnation', adding that 'In practice this means that God helps those who help themselves'.[7] Living a godly life involved a unified series of good acts which took on the character of a business enterprise. For many reformed Christians, business was the context where this took place. As it happened, worldly asceticism was well suited to accumulating wealth. Resources were put to wise use; capital grew.

Weber's thesis has been the subject of intense debate. I agree with historian Niall Ferguson, who writes that 'there are reasons to think that Weber was on to something',[8] even though the latter's judgments are questionable in detail. The psychological claims Weber made about predestination are highly speculative, and lack empirical backing; Calvinists are often notable for their confidence rather than insecurity. The significant effect of this type of Protestant Christianity was not that it generated worry about one's eternal destiny but that it saw the whole of life as under God's sovereignty. Business could and should be done to the glory of God. This motivated Christians to devote themselves enthusiastically to making a success of it.

Weber also exaggerated Protestants' self-denying tendencies. The seventeenth-century Dutch spent their hard-earned money on quite luxurious possessions, like fine furniture and beautiful paintings. Their faith made them uncomfortable with their riches, even embarrassed by them, but these habits of consumption had the positive effect of stimulating the economy.[9] The Quakers believed in plain dress and a simple lifestyle, and they generally did stay true to their principles. But this did not stop them supplying the needs and wants of those who sported a more affluent lifestyle.[10] Chocolate is a luxury item especially associated with Quakers, and their shopkeepers sold a range of expensive clothes, frills and elaborate dress.

Certainly, Protestant countries in Europe tended to grow faster than Catholic ones. By 1700 the former had clearly overtaken the latter in *per capita* income, and by 1940 people in Protestant countries were on average 40% better off than people in Catholic countries.[11] American Roman Catholic thinker Michael Novak, an enthusiastic advocate of capitalism, acknowledges the existence of a long-standing Catholic anti-capitalist bias: Catholic nations have been 'long retarded in encouraging development, invention, savings, investment, entrepreneurship, and, in general, economic dynamism'.[12] Catholic attitudes towards money were 'based on pre-modern realities' and Catholic thought 'did not understand the creativity and productivity of wisely invested capital'.[13] He and several fellow-Catholics are now seeking to reverse this trend. In *The Catholic Ethic and the Spirit of Capitalism*, Novak draws on papal encyclicals of the last 100 years, starting wth *Rerum Novarum* (1891), and argues that the debate stirred by these documents has yielded a richer, more humane view of capitalism than that found in Weber.

Conversely, it cannot be assumed any longer that Protestant churches will encourage a positive immersion in the business world. Attitudes are affected by many interrelated factors: cultural context, social situation, national history and the type of theology taught in different churches. In this book I shall draw particular attention to the importance of theology, the underlying beliefs that people have about God, humanity and the world. What we are taught and what we believe have a greater impact on what we do than many of us realize.

Five key criteria

I began by calling Christian faith a power for good in the global economy when it fulfils five criteria: stimulating enterprise, reducing poverty, promoting integrity, encouraging sustainability and fostering discipleship. More about each will emerge in later chapters, but a brief description at this stage may be helpful.

Stimulating enterprise

Enterprise is the mainspring of business. The global economy never stands still. While entrepreneurs have sometimes been branded as dangerous and unscrupulous, luring others to an unpleasant fate like the pied piper of Hamelin, it is by undertaking new ventures, trying out new products, services and processes, and refining what currently exists in search of something better, that progress is made. The church should encourage entrepreneurship as a noble vocation that requires qualities of vision, passion, risk-taking, persistence and decisiveness. In demonstrating these qualities, we emulate God's character.

Reducing poverty

Business can bring people out of poverty. It can deliver them from dehumanizing and demoralizing living conditions that are an affront to their human dignity. While business is often portrayed as a selfish endeavour, in which my success is at others' expense (whether they are ousted competitors or exploited employees), this is not necessarily the case. The church should encourage a view of business with social as well as financial purposes. In making business benefit the needy, release people from poverty and transform society, we are faithful to the mission of Jesus.

Promoting integrity

Moral standards apply in business as much as any other area of life. Business is toughly competitive, and doing the right thing can be costly, but it is still a place where people of integrity can flourish. We are misled by a picture of business as an area where normal rules of behaviour don't apply, and individuals and companies live or die by the law of the jungle. The church should encourage people to do business without deception or corruption. By living integrated lives exhibiting honesty, consistency and transparency, we present ourselves as a 'living sacrifice, holy and acceptable to God' (Romans 12:1).

Encouraging sustainability

Business must be sustainable in order to survive and flourish. But sustainability has assumed new significance in recent years because of the environmental crisis that threatens the earth. While business has taken much of the blame for overexploiting the world's resources and contributing to global warming, it is starting to rise to the challenge of environmental sustainability. The church should encourage responsible stewardship. In affirming that the world is God's and God has entrusted care of his creation to humanity, we recognize that we are accountable for that stewardship.

Fostering discipleship

Business is an important and strategic place for Christian witness. Businesspeople often get to know their colleagues well, and have many opportunities to share the good news of God's love with them. Jesus commanded his disciples to 'go and make disciples of all nations' (Matthew 28:19). The emphasis should be not just on making converts (though that is an important first step) but also on fostering discipleship: teaching men and women to glorify God through being faithful followers of Jesus in the marketplace.

Sadly, some forms of Christian faith are more a hindrance than a help in the global economy. In the contemporary world, this menace takes three main forms: prosperity theology, anti-capitalist theology and the sacred–secular divide. Though very different, each wields considerable influence in global terms. But they are all distorted views which leave Christians seriously misled and poorly equipped to serve in God's world. The next chapter shows how.

2. THEOLOGY IN BUSINESS: HINDRANCE OR HELP?

Solomon is an aspiring young businessman in East Africa. He is struggling to get his company up and running but the store he runs is starting to make a small profit. He attends a Pentecostal church with vibrant worship and a wonderful gospel choir. The pastor preaches fervently that 'God will reward those who give generously'. The congregation take him at his word and, despite the extreme poverty in which most of them live, faithfully give a tithe of their meagre incomes. Solomon notices that the pastor is becoming rich, enjoying a lifestyle far more affluent than his or those of the majority of the congregation.

Laura is a successful entrepreneur in the UK. Her printing business employs a dozen people and enables her to be generous in support of local community projects. But the minister at the church she attends never seems to have a good word for business. Condemning capitalism as greed, he regularly attacks business leaders and exalts servant leadership as *the* truly Christian approach. Yet she herself seeks to exercise servant leadership in her business: going out of her way to help employees and customers, but never abdicating the responsibility to make decisions and take initiatives. Laura is becoming seriously disillusioned with the church and is starting to look for spiritual support elsewhere.

Alan works for a large accountancy firm in Australia. He has tried to apply his faith in the workplace but has more or less given up. The church he attends offers solid biblical exposition but none of it seems to relate to the balance sheets and tax returns that occupy him from Monday to Friday. When asked about a Christian view on accountancy, his vicar is non-plussed; he has nothing to say. Meanwhile Alan's colleagues are dedicated to furthering their careers by doing whatever their clients want. If that means advising them on tax avoidance and doing a little creative accounting along the way, so what? Alan finds it easier to conform to peer practice than take a moral stand on financial practices.

What unites these three examples, different though they are? Solomon, Laura and Alan are all suffering from distorted theologies – theologies taught by their church leaders.

Distorted theologies: (i) prosperity theology

Prosperity theology, also known as the prosperity gospel or the 'health and wealth' gospel, is a major hindrance globally. It has not made a major impact in the UK, but it has a pervasive allure, with its proponents claiming tens of millions of adherents worldwide. It arose in the USA after the Second World War but became popular and spread rapidly in the 1980s and 1990s. Several high-profile American preachers have championed the prosperity gospel. They include Oral Roberts, Kenneth Copeland, Kenneth Hagin, Benny Hinn and Joyce Meyer. Many are televangelists. Their influence has spread across the world, especially to Africa and parts of Asia. Christian bookshops in Nairobi and Lagos abound with books, CDs and DVDs of the 'health and wealth' genre.

Prosperity theology teaches that faithful Christians can expect God to bless them with financial prosperity. The normal Christian life includes good health and substantial wealth. Believers 'have a right to the blessings of health and wealth', and 'they can obtain these blessings through positive confessions of faith and the 'sowing of seeds' through the faithful payments of tithes and offerings.[1] This teaching is based on interpretation of biblical verses especially beloved of prosperity preachers:

- God's promise to the Israelites on the verge of the Promised Land: 'But remember the Lord your God, for it is he who gives you the power to get wealth, so that he may confirm his covenant that he swore to your ancestors, as he is doing today' (Deuteronomy 8:18).
- The prophet Malachi's exhortation to pay tithes fully: 'Bring the full tithe into the storehouse, so that there may be food in my house, and thus put me to the test, says the Lord of hosts; see if I will not open the windows of heaven for you and pour down for you an overflowing blessing' (Malachi 3:10).
- Jesus' assurance to his disciples: 'Everyone who has left houses or brothers or sisters or father or mother or children or fields, for my name's sake, will receive a hundredfold, and will inherit eternal life' (Matthew 19:29).
- John's wish for his friend Gaius: 'Beloved, I pray that all may go well with you and that you may be in good health, just as it is well with your soul' (3 John 2).

The prominence given to the last verse is particularly interesting, because it comes from a biblical book that is rarely studied. When Roberts was twenty-nine he opened his Bible at random and his eyes were drawn to 3 John 2. He decided God wanted him to be rich and on the strength of this conviction bought a Buick the next day.

Prosperity preachers are overhasty in interpreting blessing and wellbeing in financial terms; God can bless us in many different ways. Nevertheless, the passages above do form an important part of the Bible's teaching on wealth and poverty.

Material possessions are gifts from God, and he intends human beings to enjoy them. In the providence of God, some become richer than others. But the biblical material on wealth is varied, complex, and contains plenty of caveats and warnings. In the Old Testament, rich people are expected to be generous, and the godly rich usually are. When the rich flaunt their wealth and oppress the poor, they are roundly criticized. And although material possessions may be a God-given blessing, they are, in Craig Blomberg's words, 'simultaneously one of the primary means of turning human hearts away from God'.[2] In the New Testament Jesus identified this danger when he said, 'No one can serve two masters, for a slave will either hate the one or love the other. You cannot serve God and Mammon' (Matthew 6:24). Jesus' encounter with the rich young ruler (Mark 10:17–31) and the parables of the Rich Fool (Luke 12:13–21) and Dives and Lazarus (Luke 16:19–31) show that he saw money and possessions as exerting a powerful hold over people, deterring them from following him and even imperilling their prospects of salvation.

Blomberg's balanced survey of the biblical material on wealth is entitled *Neither Poverty nor Riches*. The phrase is taken from Proverbs 30:8–9, which explains why both riches and poverty are dangerous, but for different reasons: 'Give me neither poverty nor riches; feed me with the food that I need, or I shall be full, and deny you, and say, "Who is the Lord?" or I shall be poor, and steal, and profane the name of my God.' Although this passage is unusual in articulating a material mean so explicitly, its conviction that extremes of both wealth and poverty are undesirable has clear resonances among other biblical writers. It is not a balance found in the prosperity preachers, who have eyes only for the passages that suit their case.

In addition, prosperity preachers are open to the charges of naivety and cynicism. They are naive in interpreting the accumulation of wealth so unambiguously as a blessing from God. Many North American Christians are rich because of when and where they live. But televangelists become wealthy partly from their practice of demanding that others give – generously – to support their ministries. Frequently a lavish lifestyle with several houses, private jet, even a private airport, follows. When this so-called gospel is exported to the developing world, the consequences are serious. In Africa, people's state of poverty is often extreme. No amount of faith that they can muster (on its own) is likely to change that. The one group likely to benefit from prosperity theology are the self-taught, self-appointed leaders of churches who preach it – such as Solomon's pastor. Like televangelists, they stand to gain from a high-pressured insistence on full payment of tithes.

Judged by the fivefold criteria of exercising a power for good in the global economy, prosperity theology fails. It may be accompanied by an entrepreneurial attitude, but the prosperity gospel does not positively encourage that, because its emphasis is on wealth direct from God, not from human initiative. Norwegian academic Magne Supphellen has undertaken research on the impact of religious attitudes on entrepreneurial self-efficacy: specifically, the ability of owners of micro-finance businesses in the Nairobi slums to develop and succeed with their businesses.[3] He and his researchers identified three different religious perspectives: those who see their work as a calling from God; those who think that if they believe strongly enough, God will give them success; and those with a weak sense of personal agency who are fatalistic, believing that their future lies entirely in the hands of God. The first group are much the most effective handlers of micro-finance loans. Even though this is a very limited sample, these statistics suggest that prosperity theology falls short on the second criterion also: it is not reducing poverty, because it looks to quick, 'God will fix it' answers rather than encouraging people to use their God-given brains to tackle poverty with a well-focused strategy.

Prosperity theology is even more of a hindrance when we consider the other criteria. The methods of many of its leading practitioners are sufficiently dubious that their own personal integrity has been called into question. Nor is a concern for ensuring sustainability evident in their teaching. On the contrary, ready acceptance of a state of affluence often goes hand in hand with an 'end times' theology that sees the current earth as bound for destruction. With such a belief, what's the point in holding back on personal consumption?

Distorted theologies: (ii) anti-capitalist theology

Capitalism dominates the global economy, a trend reinforced by the collapse of Communist regimes in Eastern Europe in 1989. Marx thought capitalism was a necessary stage in economic development that would be replaced by communism, but capitalism outlasted its ideological foe. Even China, communist in name, is best described as a capitalist country with an authoritarian government. Capitalism is a system centrally concerned with the increase of capital – hence the word. Its key features are a commitment to economic growth, private possession of capital, personal freedom and respon-sibility, and the autonomy of the market.

While many Christians applaud the capitalist system and believe it is consistent with biblical principles, some can scarcely muster a good word for it. There is a radical theo-logical anti-capitalist critique. In the UK, two of its chief exponents are Timothy Gorringe and Wilf Wilde.[4]

Timothy Gorringe is a professor of theology at Exeter University. His 1994 *Capital and the Kingdom* is an outspoken attack on global capitalism. His biblical rallying cry is Deuteronomy 30:19: 'I call heaven and earth to witness against you this day, that I have set before you life and death, blessing and curse; therefore choose life, that you and your descendants may live.' Like the Israelites on the verge of the Promised Land, Gorringe thinks that two ways lie before us, a way of life and a way of death: 'the way of death is the prevailing economic system, built on cynicism and whistling for destruction, content to enjoy power and affluence at the expense of the Third World and future generations.'[5]

Gorringe sees the underlying assumptions and imperatives of conventional economics as leading to catastrophe. He bemoans the triumph of the ideology of self-interest, the autonomous market, and the concealed exercise of powerful forces within it. He presents the North as an exploiter and pillager, the South as the unfortunate victim. Gorringe calls for a new economic order. This would eradicate the distinction between managers and managed, make the local economy central, and abolish usury. In *Fair Shares* he calls for a socialist revival because only socialism subordinates the market to democratic control.[6]

Wilf Wilde is a development economist and former stockbroker. His *Crossing the River of Fire* mixes theology, political economy and history. By his own admission it is 'a deliberately polemical account full of not totally proven sweeping assertions'.[7] Writing in the wake of the war in Iraq, Wilde says this should be seen as 'part and parcel of an expanding Global Capitalist Empire, dominated by the USA, with Britain and other corporations [*sic*] in a vital supporting role'.[8] For him, 'empire' has entirely negative connotations of expansionist power, exploitation and control, a theme he illustrates with reference to a wide variety of countries over several different centuries.

Wilde's biblical inspiration for his critique of empire is the Gospel of Mark. He sees Jesus as 'engaging in a sustained theological and ideological attack on the old order of the collaborationist Jewish Establishment and the Roman colonial Empire'.[9] We need today a similarly apocalyptic vision to help us discern and expose imperial ideology. Because he sees the key problem of capitalism as structural inequality, the forces of capital controlling producers, he proposes a reform of companies' voting structure: that every shareholder should have equal voting rights, whatever the size of their shareholding. Wilde claims that 'My proposal would revolutionize the ownership of all publicly owned corporations at a parliamentary stroke'.[10]

In this book I myself will echo some of these criticisms of global capitalism. It is certainly a system that demonstrates abundant evidence of sinful humanity. The workings of the international economy reveal much that is selfish, cruel, cynical or manipulative: the flagrant exploitation of power by vested interests. Why, then, do I consider the overall contribution of Gorringe and Wilde (and others like them) unhelpful? There are two reasons.

First, their overall assessment of global capitalism is not fair or balanced. As Christians we should recognize and praise what is good, as well as exposing and criticizing what is bad. Can these critics not acknowledge some of the benefits of living in Western society, 'goods' it is all too easy to take for granted?

At one point Wilde does so. He writes, 'Even though I oppose global capitalism, it is the highest form of world development we have yet achieved. More people today live longer, are better fed, are better educated and have better health.'[11] Indeed they do. The advances made in the last two centuries have been enormous. Average global life expectancy at birth around 1800 was just 28.5 years. Two centuries later in 2001, it had more than doubled to 66.6 years.[12] Typhoid and cholera were virtually eliminated in nineteenth-century Europe through improvements in public health and sanitation. An unsung hero of English history is Joseph Bazalgette, the civil engineer who responded to the cholera epidemics which devastated London in 1848–9 and 1854, and the 'Great Stink' that halted Parliament in 1858. He devised an effective sewer system for central London.[13] Every time I visit a Third World city which lacks one, I am grateful for the economic culture which prized scientific ingenuity and produced a man like Bazalgette. And although it is shocking that so many countries still lack universal clean water and sanitation systems, health and life expectancy in the developing world is slowly improving. European expansion, though morally suspect in many ways, brought better medicines in its train.

Wilde continues: 'Yet the poor in our society are more marginal than ever, so are the poor worldwide.'[14] It is true that inequality between the rich and the poor has widened in recent years, both in terms of the richest and poorest countries, and the richest and poorest individuals in most countries. Salaries for the highest earners have rocketed, an issue I shall address later. But this truth should not make us think 'the rich get richer and the poor get poorer'. Most of the poor are getting richer too: only slightly richer, but this is still significant. In some countries like China, dramatic advances have taken place. Taking the widely accepted definition of poverty as managing on only $1.25 a day, 84% of Chinese were poor in 1981. Twenty-four years later, that proportion had shrunk to 16%. About 500 million people had come out of poverty.[15] This happened as the country moved in a clear capitalist direction. Brazil has also alleviated poverty significantly during the last decade. A World Bank study concluded that this was due to a mixture of market-oriented reforms and progressive social policies.[16]

Second, the condemnations of capitalism made by its keenest critics lack nuance. I struggle to find a positive remark made about any multinational company by Gorringe and Wilde. But are all these companies equally as bad as each other? Some are raising health, safety and environmental standards in the developing countries where they operate. Surely it is wrong to tar them all with the same dark brush. To evaluate the global economy aright we need detailed investigation, not dismissive generalization.

During my twenty-two years of running the Faith in Business project, I have met many Christians who are nothing like the caricature of the ruthless and greedy businessman. They are remarkably idealistic, exhibit a high degree of integrity and care deeply about the people affected by their business activities. I know many corporate executives with a strong sense of responsibility to all the different groups with which they do business: not just to themselves or their share-holders, but also to customers, employees, suppliers and the local or wider community.

An anti-capitalist theology does not help them. People like Laura are hurt and bemused by it. They are seeking to serve God and love their neighbour, often in testing and challenging environments, but they then find the entire system in which they work called into question. It is true that anti-capitalist critics often have admirable ideals: they genuinely want to see a world in which poverty is reduced, integrity is promoted and sustainability encouraged. Yet if they fail to recognize good things businesspeople are already doing, their contribution is unhelpful. They are demoralizing the troops on the front line.

The outspoken critics are not appreciative enough of the mainspring of business, the spirit of enterprise. This cannot simply be taken for granted; it needs nurturing. The vast majority of businesspeople work in small companies, each started by an aspiring entrepreneur. Entrepreneurial flair and initiative play a major part, not just in changing the fortunes of an individual, family or workforce, but also in transforming the state of a nation.

This is relevant to the most significant anti-capitalist theological movement of the last fifty years: liberation theology, which is rooted in Latin America. It began as a protest movement within the Roman Catholic Church. Taking their lead from the Exodus, and adopting a broadly Marxist analysis of society, liberation theologians protested in the name of God's 'preferential option for the poor' against the exploitative nature of global capitalism, especially as it affected Latin America. They objected to Western countries which championed free markets and democracy shoring up oppressive and undemocratic governments, even military dictatorships.

The liberation theologians promoted the formation of 'base communities' in which the poor studied the Bible in their own way, liberated from Western presuppositions. Some even advocated violence, aiming to bring about political revolution and initiate an alternative economic system. Liberation theology was at its height between 1965 and 1985 as scholars produced an impressive number of books: Gustavo Gutiérrez (Peru), Leonardo Boff (Brazil), Jon Sobrino (El Salvador), José Porfirio Miranda (Mexico), Juan Luis Segundo (Uruguay) and – the one Protestant among them – José Miguez Bonino (Argentina).[17]

A generation later, what is the lasting impact of their work? Smaller than might have been expected – and not just because many of them got into trouble with the papacy. Latin America has changed, in many ways for the better: most countries have grown in prosperity and replaced military governments with democratic ones. Improvement has not come through Marxist economics. Today, Chile's economy stands out for its stability, relative lack of corruption, and overall health. Ironically, the foundations for this were laid in the latter years of the oppressive Pinochet regime, which introduced privatisation and reduced inflation.

Progress in South America has also occurred through increased small-scale entrepreneurial activity, in which Protestants have played a prominent role. Studies in Brazil and Chile by sociologist David Martin show that conversion to Protestantism often brings about a cultural revolution.[18] Individuals who join these Protestant churches – mainly Pentecostal – gain a heightened sense of their identity. They come to see themselves not just as 'the poor', but as having a God-given dignity which helps them believe they can change their lot. So their behaviour often shifts in a disciplined, thrifty, enterprising direction, the crucial characteristics noted by Weber.

The German theologian Jürgen Moltmann, of whom I shall say more shortly, was a fellow-traveller with the liberation theologians during the 1970s, until some accused him of being a Western 'bourgeois' theologian at a conference in Mexico City in 1977. Moltmann now makes the fascinating observation:

> In some places the evangelical Pentecostal movement is
> more successful than the Catholic liberation theologians
> and base communities in making 'the poor' the determining

subjects of their own experience of God and their own lives, not merely instructing them but also awakening them to new life. The Latin American Pentecostal movement could become the true criticism and continuation of liberation theology.[19]

Distorted theologies: (iii) the sacred–secular divide

A third affliction of the church worldwide is the *sacred–secular divide*. The phrase has been popularized by Mark Greene, Director of the London Institute for Contemporary Christianity – even to the point of calling it SSD for short.[20] This is the habit of dividing reality into two spheres, the sacred and the secular, and keeping them firmly apart. So Christianity is seen as relevant to church, family and local community, the personal and private. But it is seen as irrelevant to the rest of life, especially the tough, competitive world of business and politics. Introduce Christian language and Christian standards there, and you're in for trouble.

The sources for this sacred–secular divide are various. There are historical and cultural factors. In the USA, it tends to parallel the separation made between church and state. Even in Western countries with an established church, like the UK, pluralism is now the dominant reality. Pluralist societies are made up of people with diverse views, outlooks and backgrounds: ethnic, religious and political. For business and political leaders, this makes it difficult to pursue a shared vision and an agreed ethical approach. Multinational companies that are by definition multicultural have a real challenge on this score, though some rise to it admirably. The accepted wisdom is to look for common ground (a vision which can be accepted by all) and to give distinctive religious approaches short shrift, either because they are likely to be divisive or because they set the bar unreasonably high.

The reluctance of many businesspeople to be open about their faith and advocate a Christian approach to business also reflects the lack of encouragement and support that they receive from their local churches. Greene provides plenty of evidence, statistical and anecdotal, which illustrates this; my own experience (national and international) confirms it. There is a shortage of Christian teaching on whole-life discipleship – that is, in-depth biblical application of what it means to be a faithful follower of Christ in every part of life. There is little emphasis on Christian witness in the workplace: local churches encourage you to bring your next-door neighbour to an evangelistic event, when you probably know your colleague at the next desk or till much better. There is a lack of willingness in local fellowships to talk openly about issues at work, especially situations of stress or temptation. Without support from people in their church, it is easy for Christians in business like Alan to live compartmentalized lives, bowing to peer pressure, fitting in with the corporate ethos and making the small but significant compromises which eventually result in their erecting a sacred–secular divide without ever consciously intending it.

This sacred–secular divide is sometimes given a theological justification: that in the political and economic realms of life God accommodates himself to the sinful character of humanity. He restrains force with the threat of force – as seen in Paul's teaching that the governing authorities are God-given and do not bear the sword in vain (Romans 13:1–7). Jesus said, 'Give to the emperor the things that are the emperor's, and to God the things that are God's' (Mark 13:17). On the surface, this seems to justify a demarcation of life into two realms.[21] The realm where, typically, Caesar rules is a tough, competitive world in which only the fittest survive and reason, pragmatism and self-interest reign supreme. Many people's experience of business fits this description. It contrasts with other areas of life, such as marriage and the family, where God's radical commandment to love (spelled out in Jesus' Sermon on the Mount) can be followed more directly and the need for self-sacrifice has obvious relevance.

I believe this view is based on a misunderstanding of Jesus. In circumstances where his enemies were snaring him with a trick question about paying taxes, he was trying to make his questioners do two things: think anew about what they did owe to Caesar, and recognize that their primary allegiance was to God. Jesus saw God's rule as extending over the whole of life in an integrated way. True, discerning God's will is not always easy, and the murky circumstances in which many businesspeople operate mean there may not always be a perfect solution. But the Bible's call to be holy challenges our all-too-human tendency to consider the imperfect normal and acceptable.

In general, however, the sacred–secular divide is reinforced by a lack of theology rather than the imposition of a particular theology. Few theological seminaries worldwide teach a positive theology of work or have members of faculty inclined and equipped to speak positively about business. This is reflected in those who go on to lead local churches. Sermons rarely engage with the real world of estate agents, lorry drivers and restaurant owners – even though the Bible is peppered with stories featuring people in very specific occupations.

Where Christians allow a clear division to develop between the sacred and secular, disastrous results often follow. Sadly, high-profile professing Christians are regularly implicated in business and financial scandals that hit the headlines. In 2002 the massive profits of US energy company Enron, named by Fortune as America's most innovative company for six consecutive years, were revealed to be the creation of institutional, systematic and creative accounting fraud. The CEO, Kenneth Lay, was a self-proclaimed Southern Baptist, who worked tirelessly for numerous charitable causes in the Houston area. He said that the company's ethical code (impressive, by all accounts) was based on Christian values.[22] Because he died suddenly soon after his conviction on eleven counts of conspiracy and fraud, he was never able to explain how he squared his business practice with his apparently exemplary private life. It is similarly disturbing that Bernie Ebbers, the CEO of WorldCom, now serving a twenty-five-year sentence for conspiracy and fraud, taught in the Sunday school at his church in Brookhaven, Mississippi. One can only surmise that compartmentalization had taken an extreme form in their cases: that they were operating by the maxim that, in business, 'anything goes'.

A godly calling

The Reformer Martin Luther's doctrine of calling offers a more positive theological response. Through his personal reading of Romans he discovered Paul's theology of justification by grace through faith alone. This and his subsequent break with Rome led him to rail against the monastic life which, he believed, had led him and others astray. He affirmed the equal status of all Christians, emphasizing the great variety of occupations in which it is possible to work hard and serve God. The mother suckling her baby, the maid brandishing her broom and the magistrate passing sentence were doing something of real value if they performed these tasks in response to God's command and to his glory. Calling became a basic category for understanding Christian life in the Lutheran and wider Protestant tradition. The primary calling, as is clear from numerous New Testament passages, is to respond to God's offer of salvation. The secondary calling, which Luther based on his interpretation of 1 Corinthians 7:17–20, is to accept as God-given the duties that come through occupational, social and family positions, and fulfil them wholeheartedly.

Some see the revival of this notion of godly calling as the main hope for reversing the sacred–secular divide. We have already seen that a strong sense of calling provides the most powerful of three different theological motivations found among small-scale Kenyan businesspeople. I myself know leading bankers in the city of London who understand their work in terms of their Christian vocation. They believe that by serving in the financial markets they are contributing to the common good, helping developing economies to grow, and providing the necessary infrastructure for world trade and global investment.

Yet I wonder if some businesspeople, including bankers, are too easily satisfied by 'calling' as the underlying rationale for all that they do. Yes, God calls people into business, but doesn't he also call us to a discerning critique of current business practices? Calling should be the start of an in-depth engagement of Christian faith with the global economy; instead, naming it often seems to end the discussion. There is more to be mined from the rich resources of biblical theology.

Hope for the world

This book is structured around the theme of hope, for three reasons.

2008 was the year of Hope 08; many churches and Christian organizations around the UK took part in this national initiative. Numerous events, programmes and projects were organized under the title of 'Hope'. This led me to think: how can we express our faith in a way that communicates hope? My response was to put together a display in text and picture summarizing what Christians believe. I presented Christian belief as a storyline, the saga of salvation history, which I see as a drama in seven acts. Anyone who came into St Philip's Church on Mill Road, Cambridge, during that year (believer, half-believer and unbeliever alike) will have seen that display.

The remaining chapter headings of this book correspond to the seven acts of the drama. I find that this provides an excellent structure for relating Christian faith to every area of life, business included. Each act in the drama of salvation – from creation and fall right through to our future hope – has implications for the world of business. Every important, topical and contentious business issue finds its place somewhere in the biblical story. In these pages you will find discussions of limited liability, executive pay, fair treatment of employees and the paying of bribes to win international contracts. And a balanced biblical theology brings to prominence the five key criteria mentioned earlier: stimulating enterprise, reducing poverty, promoting integrity, ensuring sustainability and fostering discipleship.

2008 was also a year when I returned to a book that I had first read many years earlier: Jürgen Moltmann's *A Theology of Hope*. I was prompted to do so because Moltmann had accepted an invitation to be our Ridley Hall Moule lecturer in 2009. He duly visited Ridley to give this special lecture and it was a great pleasure to meet this distinguished and delightful man.

Back in the 1960s, *A Theology of Hope* was an epoch-making book. Moltmann played a major role in reviving hope as a key category in Christian living. He wrote the memorable words: 'From first to last, and not merely in the epilogue, Christianity is eschatology, is hope, forward looking and forward moving, and therefore also revolutionizing and transforming the present.'[23] Yet though Moltmann outlines an impressive theology of hope, its application to the workplace and economic life is undeveloped in that book. This is despite Moltmann's interest in work, as revealed in his later writings.[24] But he didn't bring together the two strands of hope and work in any systematic way. This left me wondering whether the task had been left for someone else. Could it be me?

Furthermore, hope is especially crucial in the context of economic recession, which we have experienced in the UK and many other countries since the global crisis of 2007–9. Without hope, the expectation of a better future, there is little prospect we will have the positive attitudes that will contribute to bringing that future about. Belief that genuine improvement is impossible, and that God both cares about our contribution and inspires our best efforts, is all-important.

Another major theological work on hope is Tom Wright's *Surprised by Hope*. Wright believes passionately, as I do, that belief in the resurrection and our hope of a new heaven and a new earth should have a transforming effect on the work we do now. He writes:

> What you do with your body in the present matters, because God has a great future in store for it . . . What you *do* in the present – by painting, preaching, singing, sewing, praying, teaching, building hospitals, digging wells, loving your neighbour as yourself – all these things *will last into God's future.*[25]

A few pages later, he makes a similar point:

> Every act of love, gratitude and kindness; every work of art or music inspired by the love of God and delight in the

beauty of his creation; every minute spent teaching a severely handicapped child to read or to walk; every act of care and nurture, of comfort and support, for one's fellow human beings, and for that matter one's fellow non-human creatures; and of course every prayer, all Spirit-led teaching, every deed which spreads the gospel, builds up the church, embraces and embodies holiness rather than corruption, and makes the name of Jesus honoured in the world – all of this will find its way, through the resurrecting power of God, into the new creation which God will one day make.[26]

This is an engaging and inspiring picture that Wright portrays. But in my view both descriptions suffer from a lack of examples from a commercial context. Is there really nothing of an entrepreneurial or wealth-creating nature that that will have a place in God's new creation? The positive role that business plays in the outworking of God's purposes goes unnoticed.

This book is an attempt to make good such deficiencies, to complete what has been lacking in the account that many others give of Christian hope. It is an account of what Christians believe that is geared unashamedly to the world inhabited by businesspeople. Why are entrepreneurs so dear to the heart of God? What is the relevance of Ezekiel's prophecy against Tyre for Western Europe today? How is Jesus, 'a friend of prostitutes', an inspiration for life-changing business enterprises in India and Kenya? When is it right to resign on a point of moral principle? Are cooperatives a more 'Christian' form of corporate structure?

Read on to discover more.

3. LAUNCHED IN HOPE: CREATION AND ENTREPRENEURSHIP

The word 'hope' does not appear in the biblical story of creation. But it is evident that God invested a great deal of hope in creating planet earth. The narratives of Genesis 1 and 2 abound with a sense of purpose and direction. God creates the world in a systematic way, each stage a logical precursor to the next. God periodically assessed what he had done and 'saw that it was good' (Genesis 1:3, 10, 12, 18, 25). It is good because it is fit for purpose; there is a God-given goal for each aspect of his creation. For example, the sun and moon are made to provide light for day and night respectively (1:14–16); plants are created to provide food for both humans and animals (1:29–30).

Privilege and task

In Genesis 1 and 2, God's positive intentions for the world are largely focused on human beings, who are the pinnacle of his creation. This is shown by the resemblance between God and humanity: 'So God created humanity in his image, in the image of God he created them; male and female he created them' (Genesis 1:27). While the content of this divine image is never defined, it gives human beings status and authority. We occupy an intermediate position between the Creator and the rest of creation. Verse 26 states: 'let them have dominion over the fish of the sea, and over the birds of the air, and over the cattle, and over all the wild animals of the earth, and over every creeping thing that creeps upon the earth.' Verse 28 reaffirms this.

Genesis 1 and 2 comprise two accounts, one starting at 1:1 and the second at 2:4. The creation of man is described afresh in 2:7: 'the Lord God formed man from the dust of the ground, and breathed into his nostrils the breath of life, and the man became a living being.' In the second account, the emphasis is not so much on human beings' privileged position in relation to creation as their responsibility for looking after it. 'The Lord God took the man and put him in the garden of Eden to till it and keep it' (Genesis 2:15). The word 'till' has its roots in the Hebrew word 'serve'. Bishop James Jones comments: 'Adam who is hewn from the earth is called to serve the very earth from which he was formed.'[1] Human beings impose order and ensure productivity by disciplined cultivation – gardening, no less. Along with cultivation comes the task of classification. I love the picture of God bringing the animals and birds to Adam to 'see what he would call them' (2:19). God could have given these creatures names and told Adam what they were. Instead he allows the man to name them himself.

A Ridley student, Sarah, previously worked as a botanist at Kew Gardens. She classified different kinds of daisy, even having the satisfaction of naming a couple (there are about 25,000 different types!). So she too was involved in labelling God's creation. I told her that she was a true successor to Adam, and even more so (as a woman) to Eve: God made Eve to be Adam's helper (2:20), and the task of classifying flora follows on from naming animals.

For much of history, most people have farmed the land. In a subsistence economy, people live off the land; in many developing countries this is still true to some extent. But in industrialized economies, the small minority who work the land trade with others who have neither time, inclination nor land to feed themselves. So the fulfilment of God's command to Adam now has a commercial dimension: where once existed the primeval garden, we cannot escape the reality of business. Farmers sell to markets and supermarkets. The deliberately named Eden Project in Cornwall is both an educational charity, teaching visitors about the natural world, and a money-spinning social enterprise.

Work and rest

Let's return to Genesis 1. We have seen the regular interruption of the text with the comment, 'And God saw that it was good.' This reaches a climax in Genesis 1:31: 'God saw everything that he had made, and indeed, it was very good. And there was evening and there was morning, the sixth day.'

The creation when completed was not just good; it was *very* good. God takes immense satisfaction in what he has done, delighting in the product of his ingenuity. The design entailed in God's feat of cosmic architecture embodies a profound wisdom. Proverbs 8 expresses this by picturing wisdom as God's master craftsman:

> When he established the heavens, I was there,
> . . . when he marked out the foundations of the earth,
> then I was beside him, like a master worker,
> and I was daily his delight,
> rejoicing before him always,
> rejoicing in his inhabited world
> and delighting in the human race.
> (Proverbs 8:27–31)

This combination of joy and delight is deeply expectant. God delights in the human race at its beginning. The stage is set for an epic drama.

After the six 'days' of concentrated work, God rests. The first creation account ends: 'And on the seventh day God finished the work that he had done, and he rested on the seventh day from all the work that he had done. So God blessed the seventh day and hallowed it, because on it God rested from all the work that he had done in creation' (Genesis 2:2–3). God sets a limit on his own creative activity. His work is not over; he is not like an absentee chairman on an indefinite holiday in the Bahamas. The main focus of his activity will shortly turn to the providential work of upholding the finite creatures he has made.[2]

God rests not for his own benefit but because he wishes to confer his rest on us. God's activity in creation is described as work, and we have already seen that he gives human beings plenty of work – purposeful productive activity – to do. As human beings made in the likeness of God, we 'image' God by working. But there is a time for rest as well as for work, and God sets us an example in both.

That the sabbath rest is intended for us to emulate is affirmed twice in the Torah. The fourth commandment, 'Remember the Sabbath day, and keep it holy', is grounded in the fact that 'in six days the Lord made heaven and earth, the sea, and all that is in them, but rested the seventh day; therefore the Lord blessed the Sabbath day and consecrated it' (Exodus 20:8, 11). Deuteronomy 5:12–16 emphasizes that the Israelites are to allow their slaves rest as well – mindful that they themselves were slaves in Egypt.

Taking a day of rest is important for many reasons. It allows us to worship God with fellow-believers, to spend time with family, to recover energy and to listen to what God is saying to us. Although it is not easy keeping the sabbath in increasingly secularized societies where Sunday (the Christian form of the sabbath) has become a day like any other, shops and sport offering a seductive appeal, we ignore this God-ordained rhythm at our peril.[3]

As part of this weekly pause, there is an important place for looking back over our work and taking satisfaction in it. Although work has frustrations, cul-de-sacs and failures, seeing the fruit of our labours brings genuine pleasure. If God's example is anything to go by, we should feel free to enjoy that. Unfortunately, many of us work so hard that we do not pause to enjoy the completion of one assignment before we pass breathlessly on to the next.

John Lovatt, the managing director of a ceramics firm in the Potteries, has written these perceptive words:

> The big moment for the development engineer is after the months of building to stand back, take a deep breath and press the green button. If it works (or rather, when it eventually works), it will of course be allowed to run for several minutes, whereas a few seconds were all that was strictly necessary. Those minutes of Sabbath rejoicing are not a luxury – they are an essential part of the creative process. There are many more examples of the Sabbath principle already in unconscious use in industry, and they should be recognised and encouraged. Farmers leaning over the gate chewing over the situation, salesmen opening the champagne to celebrate a large order, athletes releasing the tension by punching the air: all these complete the process, and bring the peace and contentment which is God's gift of the Sabbath.[4]

Some might object that this period of reflecting on work well done is better assigned to Friday or Saturday evening rather than Sunday; God's designation of his creation as 'very good' is located at the end of the sixth day. But when it happens is less important than that it happens at all. We may think we don't have time for such a luxury, but it is actually crucial to our welfare. Sabbath rejoicing is a priceless principle for busy businesspeople.

God the entrepreneur

The Bible uses many powerful metaphors about God, appealing to our imaginations and making connections to our everyday experience. Alongside other images of God as, for example, father and lover, numerous occupational images are used to describe him. The Australian theologian Robert Banks has carried out a fascinating exploration in *God the Worker: Journeys into the Heart, Mind and Imagination of God.* He lists sixteen different images which he clusters in pairs: composer and performer; metalworker and potter; garment-maker and dresser; gardener and orchardist; farmer and winemaker; shepherd and pastoralist; tentmaker and camper; builder and architect.[5]

Among these images, two in particular speak of God's activity as Creator. As a potter, he 'moulds' and 'forms'. The God who created the heavens 'fashioned the earth and made it' (Isaiah 45:18). God forms the animals and birds out of the ground (Genesis 2:19). Above all, he moulds human beings, prompting the confession:

> Yet, O Lord, you are our Father;
> we are the clay, and you are the potter:
> we are the work of your hand.
> (Isaiah 64:8)

In Jeremiah 18 and 19, the potter image is also used of God's prerogative to remake the clay and break the pot. He has the right and the ability to make something new.

God is also seen as a gardener, planting the first garden in Genesis 2. The description of Eden speaks wonders of God's generous provision and love of beauty – the trees were 'pleasant to the eye'. But the garden also needs to be worked: God does not hand everything to us on a plate.

Need we be confined to these particular biblical images in speaking of God in occupational terms? Like Banks, I think not. The images used in the Bible retain considerable power, but where appropriate, we can make other comparisons from our contemporary work environment which express similar ideas and concerns.[6] By disciplined use of the imagination, we can communicate aspects of God's character in fresh ways.

One role in the business world that captures part of God's character is that of the entrepreneur. By origin the word is of course French, a point possibly lost on George W. Bush, who allegedly said to Tony Blair: 'The problem with the French is that they have no word for entrepreneur.'[7] The French economist Jean-Baptiste Say (1767–1832), whose masterpiece *A Treatise on Political Economy* deserves to rank with Smith's *The Wealth of Nations*, popularized the word in the early nineteenth century. He defined an entrepreneur as one who undertakes an enterprise, notably a contractor who acts as intermediary between capital and labour, and shifts economic resources from lower into higher productivity. As Professor Edward Younkins puts it:

> Say emphasized the vital and creative roles of entrepreneur in the economy as forecaster, project appraiser and risk taker. He saw that effective entrepreneurs must possess the moral qualities of judgment and perseverance, and also have knowledge of the world.[8]

In the early twentieth century, the Austrian economist Joseph Schumpeter (1883–1950) was the shrewdest student and most prominent advocate of entrepreneurship. He stressed the role of entrepreneurs as innovators: they devised new products and methods of production, often using new technology; they created new forms of organization and even conjured up new markets.

God, as portrayed in Genesis 1–2, exemplifies much of what Say and Schumpeter celebrate. This God creates something radically new: he is a true innovator. He exercises his wisdom in making a wonderful world with rich potential. He is blessed with superabundant knowledge and sees into the future. But he knows that he is taking a huge risk: a risk largely associated with the human beings to whom he entrusts responsibility for the earth's welfare. God will certainly need the qualities of judgment and perseverance to keep the enterprise on track.[9]

Obviously, every analogy has its limitations. That of entrepreneur tells us only so much about God. We need overtly biblical images to fill out our understanding. God's foreknowledge vastly exceeds that of even the most prescient human entrepreneur. But many of the characteristics fit. In an age when entrepreneurs have a more important role than ever, it could be a very timely image of God for Christians to use in their witness.

The fall and rise of entrepreneurs

Interestingly, Schumpeter believed that the success of capitalism would lead to a form of corporatism and a fostering of values hostile to capitalism, especially among intellectuals. A social climate would develop that discouraged rather than encouraged entrepreneurs. This happened in the UK during the period 1950–80. Entrepreneurs had a bad reputation. They were dangerous visionaries with egotistical drives, impatient to acquire wealth, ready to take moral short cuts: they were ruthlessly out to eliminate the competition. In his autobiography, Richard Branson tells how:

[i]n the 1970s, when we set up Virgin Records, no one in the
UK used the word 'entrepreneur' any more. Or if they did,
they considered it something unsavoury. A business man
running a number of firms was seen as a 'chancer' – the
television comic stereotype was Del Boy, the wheeler-dealer
on the outside of the law, in *Only Fools and Horses*. In the early
days, I was regularly dismissed as a 'Del Boy' myself . . .[10]

Attitudes have changed. Branson himself, with his informal,
unconventional image but clear commitment to giving the
customer value for money, whether selling records, air flights
or train rides, played a significant part in improving entrepreneurs' reputation. So did Anita Roddick, founder of
Body Shop International, which produces natural-ingredient
cosmetics that avoid testing on animals, and developed the
idea of corporate social responsibility long before it became
commonplace.

The image of entrepreneurs has improved; many are
known for their indefatigability, integrity and ability to inspire
other people. They are no longer treated with disdain by
academics. After 1970 a revolution of attitudes took place at
Cambridge University, as many innovative ideas with commercial application developed from university departments'
research laboratories and the two richest colleges, Trinity and
St John's, used land owned on the edge of the city to provide
a home for fledgling information technology, biotechnology
and pharmaceutical companies – at the Cambridge Science
Park and St John's Innovation Centre.[11]

Vancouver, Canada, another beehive of entrepreneurial
activity, is home to the Entrepreneurial Leaders Organization (ELO), founded by businessman and academic Rick
Goossen, whose vision is to equip, connect and inspire Christian entrepreneurial leaders. The ELO carries out an ongoing

research process interviewing Christian entrepreneurs, the outcome of which is an annual publication entitled *Entrepreneurial Leaders: Reflections on Faith and Work*.[12] These books document interviews with entrepreneurs from Canada, the USA and the UK, and are intended as an instruction for aspiring Christian entrepreneurs. Goossen aims to provide a platform for experienced practitioners to inspire a younger generation.

Not surprisingly, 100 individuals spread through five books of interviews exhibit a fair degree of variety. Yet there are clear common threads. In his introduction to volume 4, Gordon Smith comments how these are people of hope rather than cynicism. They are 'entrepreneurs who through their creativity, innovation, and persistence, model what it means to live with hope'.[13] He continues:

> An entrepreneur is one who sees reality clearly – has a good read on the circumstances; but the entrepreneur is also one who can see possibilities, connections, and the ways in which innovation and creativity can alter that reality. People of hope are not naïve; it is merely that they do not acquiesce in the status quo.[14]

This enables them to thrive in times of chaos or recession. If one market closes down, the entrepreneur thinks about what new markets might emerge; if a product becomes outdated, the entrepreneur considers the next product that might replace it. Schumpeter called this capacity not only to embrace change positively but to provoke it by challenging the status quo 'creative destruction'.[15]

In the third volume, for which I wrote an introduction, I was struck by the *passion* energizing many of the interviewees. Here are two examples.

- Paul Verhoeff, President of ISO, a flooring installation company: 'You need to lead with passion. If the leader of a company is not passionate about what the business can do, the kind of service it can provide, and how it can grow, then there is no way the rest of the staff will catch the passion. Passion starts at the top and runs downhill.'[16]
- Reg Petersen, Chairman of Versa-Care, a retirement home business: 'Entrepreneurship is my passion, and God created that passion in me for a purpose. I am called to fulfil that purpose . . . We looked for people who had a passion for the well-being of others – that was the key issue. Each needed to have a caring heart and a passion for service.'[17]

Another businessman featured in the book is Terry Smith, President of Smith Gardens, a wholesale flower distributor based in Bellingham, Washington State. Terry's enthusiasm was as evident when I met him in person as it is on paper: 'I know God wired me as an entrepreneur in my mother's womb. It's back to DNA: He hard-wired me to be passionate, creative, adventuresome, committed and encouraging.'[18]

A Ridley Hall conference on entrepreneurship in March 2009 certainly revealed plenty of entrepreneurially minded Christians who were in good heart. Although the event happened in the wake of the global financial crisis, they were undeterred. Banks may have been lending less, but entrepreneurs have ways of finding the investment finance they need, and for small-scale ventures, family and friends often provide the initial outlay. Entrepreneurship is an ongoing social necessity, even – indeed especially – during an economic downturn. The conference provided the opportunity both to gain mutual encouragement from kindred spirits and to draw inspiration from the God who gave them their creative juices.

Subduing the earth

Embedded in the first creation story are two phrases that have proved extremely controversial. We have already noted one in passing: human beings are allowed to 'have dominion' over other living creatures (Genesis 1:26, 28). They are also given permission to '[b]e fruitful and multiply, and fill the earth and subdue it'. These notions of dominion and subjugation have come under strong critical scrutiny in the light of the environmental crisis that has emerged over recent decades.

In 1967, American historian Lynn White wrote an influential essay entitled 'The Historic Roots of our Ecologic Crisis'. He claimed that because of its role in the rise of modern science and technology, 'Christianity bears a huge burden of guilt' for the present situation. Christianity established a dualism of man and nature, and insisted that it is God's will that man exploit nature for his own ends.[19]

Scottish ecologist Ian McHarg was even more outspoken when he wrote that the Genesis story, by its insistence on dominion and subjugation of nature, encourages the most exploitative and destructive instincts in humanity. 'Indeed, if one seeks licence for those who would increase radioactivity, create canals and harbours with atomic bombs, employ poisons without constraint, or give consent to the bulldozer mentality, there could be no better injunction than this text' (Genesis 1:26, 28).[20]

Christians need to be careful how they respond to such accusations. Some seek to dismiss White's charge by pointing out that ecological problems also exist in parts of the world where the Judeo-Christian tradition has had negligible influence, or that Genesis 1 should not be read in isolation from Genesis 2, with its greater emphasis on serving and caring attitudes towards the earth. Both responses are valid but inadequate. We need a more searching appraisal both of the texts deemed offensive and of the human exploits manifest in the Industrial Revolution, which has contributed to global warming during the last 250 years.

With regard to Genesis 1:26–28, it is important to be honest in our exegesis and admit that the Hebrew words 'subdue' and 'have dominion' are quite violent in tone. The verb 'have dominion' is translated elsewhere in the Old Testament as 'tread' or 'trample on', while the verb 'subdue' is used of bringing enemies of war into subjection: a clear implication that, if the earth is to satisfy human needs, considerable force needs to be used. It is sentimental nonsense to imagine that this is unnecessary. Pests must be controlled, wilderness needs to be tamed and water has to be found.

God has created a world full of remarkable resources for men and women to put to good use. Most of these resources require some process of extraction, conversion and refinement before they can be of benefit. Mineral deposits lie deep beneath the earth's surface; colossal effort with significant danger is involved in hewing and hauling them upwards. In the story of Israel, part of the appeal of the Promised Land is that it is a 'good' land 'whose stones are iron and from whose hills you may mine copper' (Deuteronomy 8:9). Job, possibly the oldest book in the Bible, contains a fascinating description of the tough world of mining:

> Surely there is a mine for silver, and a place
>   for gold to be refined.
> Iron is taken out of the earth, and copper is
>   smelted from ore.

Miners put an end to darkness,
and search out to the farthest bound
the ore in gloom and deep darkness.
They open shafts in a valley away
from human habitation;
they are forgotten by travellers,
they sway suspended, remote from people . . .
(Job 28:1–4)

Powering electricity

Although the mining of metals goes back a long way, it could be argued that the rich resources of the earth were actually *under*exploited for many millions of years. God's giving of responsibility to human beings included the possibility that they would fail to make the most of the world he had made, with sources of energy lying dormant and untapped beneath the earth's surface. All this changed with the Industrial Revolution. Coal mining provided the fuel for steam engines, which powered manufacturing machinery, as well as railways and steamships. The first oil well in Europe (in Poland) was drilled in 1853, the first in the USA (in Pennsylvania) in 1859. The extraction of natural gas followed rapidly.

Meanwhile, scientists were making revolutionary advances in their understanding of chemistry and electricity. In 1823, British manufacturer James Muspratt started mass producing soda for glass and soap, using a process developed by the French chemist Nicolas Leblanc in 1787. During the nineteenth century Volta, Ampere, Faraday and Edison all made significant discoveries as electricity changed from a subject of scientific curiosity into an essential feature of modern living. It was first used to light streets and public buildings in the 1870s and the first central power station began operating in London in 1882. Since then electricity's uses – fuelled by a ready supply of coal, oil and natural gas – seem to know no end. Try making a list of items around your house that use electric power!

We are now aware that this massive use of fossil fuels has come at immense cost to the environment. Since the Industrial Revolution began around 1750, the amount of carbon in the atmosphere has increased by nearly 30%: an additional 600,000 gigatons, with a further increase of around 6 gigatons each year. Although a small minority of scientists disagree, there is little doubt that emission of greenhouse gases is a major factor behind global warming. The Intergovernmental Panel on Climate Change (IPCC) has argued the case since 1990, with its 2007 report stating: 'Warming of the climate system is unequivocal, as is now evident from observations of increases in global average air and ocean temperatures, widespread melting of snow and ice, and rising global average sea level.'[21]

In the face of such alarming statistics, which have severe implications for people living in low-lying countries threatened by flooding, the world is bedevilled by two polarized and unhelpful reactions. These responses were evident both at the 2009 Copenhagen climate summit and in the recriminations that followed the failure of participating countries to make binding commitments to any meaningful measures.

The first response is to appeal to the principle of uncertainty and dispute the evidence for global warming caused by human activity. This was evident in the reasons given by President Bush for his administration's unwillingness to ratify the 1997 Kyoto Protocol, a modest international agreement for cutting greenhouse gas emissions. Bush maintained that 'we do not know how much effect natural fluctuations in climate may have had on warming. We do not know how much our climate could, or will change in the future. We do not know how fast change will occur, or even how some of our actions could impact it'.[22] This attitude is not as prevalent as it was in the USA, but is still widespread; nor is it confined to that country. The problem is that uncertainty looks as if it is being used as an excuse for inertia. High users of electricity powered by fossil fuels (along with major shareholders in coal, oil and gas companies) would much prefer to maintain the status quo.

The second reaction is to argue for a wholesale transfer from fossil fuels to sources of renewable energy. This is often accompanied by a failure to appreciate the benefits that have come from technological development and a view of the Industrial Revolution as an unmitigated disaster. The fact is that our forbears who developed the use of oil, gas and electricity immeasurably improved the quality of our lives. Electricity drastically decreases the dangers of darkness; it facilitates the operation of hospitals and makes possible global communication.

Exercising dominion over the earth is not primarily destructive. It produces benefits we would be foolish and ungrateful to take for granted. Christianity's significant part in the scientific and technological development pioneered in the West in recent centuries should redound to its credit rather than be a matter for shame. The tragedy is that benefits have been shared so inequitably; 1.4 billion people worldwide still suffer from lack of electric power in their homes. In any case, the original developers of industrial technology were largely unaware of the long-term environmental effects of their actions. It is easy to be wise in retrospect.

Nevertheless, now that we know what we do about global warming, it is irresponsible to continue as before. In this polarized debate, Mark McAllister, the Christian former CEO of Fairfield Energy, an upstream oil producer in the North

Sea, offers a constructive voice. His argument has three main planks and is notable for its clear theological rationale.

First, he argues that:

> [h]ydrocarbon fossil fuels, especially crude oil, represent an incredible concentration of energy in a highly portable form. The exploitation of these resources has led to a phase of wealth creation unparalleled in the history of the human race. For Christians, such provision indicates the providence of God, for which we should be thankful and act in stewardship of God's precious resources. The displacement of fossil fuels by other energy sources is no simple matter. Both the benefits of fossil fuels and the difficulty in replacing them must be acknowledged in order to address these important issues in a balanced and transparent way.[23]

Second, fossil fuels are a finite resource that will one day run out, and so, not least as a responsibility under God to the developing world:

> Governments must actively encourage the development of renewable energy sources. The wealth required to be able to pursue these alternative forms of energy has been made possible by the era of fossil fuels, but it will take concerted will and effort to direct sufficient resources for the technological advances required to harness renewable sources on the scale necessary to address adequately the energy requirements of the whole world.[24]

Third, and in the meantime, energy efficiency must be pursued with vigour. Christians should set an example, living lifestyles of 'modest demand'. Remaining fossil fuel resources should be efficiently developed, since 'the time and wealth required to develop renewable energy sources can only be provided by the continued employment of oil, gas and coal'.[25]

McAllister is arguing for a phased development from fossil fuels to renewable sources of energy. Clearly, there is scope for argument about how rapid that should be and what is an appropriate mix of 'renewables' – for example, hydro-electric, sun, wind, geothermal and biomass. In this debate nuclear power occupies a special place: more sustainable than fossil fuels, free of carbon emissions, but with its own problems of waste disposal and the potential for dangerous accidents. However, even agreement on the wisdom of a gradual transition in energy sources appears elusive in the current international climate. In particular, there is need for an urgent reappraisal by the two countries that are the largest emitters of carbon dioxide emissions: China, with 22.3%, and the USA with 19.9%.[26] They are also the two largest users of coal, the most damaging fossil fuel in terms of its environmental effects: 68% of China's electricity is supplied by coal and 45% of the USA's.

If human beings underexploited the world's resources for much of its history, it is now clear that for 200 years we have *over*exploited them. This shows how difficult it is to be a wise steward of God's resources. We need to draw on the wisdom of God himself. The passage on mining cited earlier, Job 28, leads in precisely this direction. After further detail on the miners' exploits (28:9–11), Job asks: 'But where shall wisdom be found? And where is the place of understanding?' His answer is in 'the fear of the Lord, that is wisdom' (Job 28:12, 28).

Renewable energy

God in creation made a wonderful world and provides a supreme example in his work, his rest and his inventiveness. He bestowed on human beings the formidable responsibility of taking care of his creation and putting God-given resources to best possible use. Entrepreneurs play a crucial role in this. The overexploitation of global resources in recent centuries is putting a special onus on social entrepreneurs who can make the most of opportunities provided by renewable energy.

Andrew Tanswell is a Christian, an engineer and management consultant who was Executive Director of Micah Challenge UK before founding ToughStuff, a social enterprise which employs over 100 people and produces solar-powered energy solutions for some of the 1.4 billion people living without access to electricity.[27] Their solar panels, LED lamps and battery packs were designed following market research and field studies in Africa to meet the continent's specific needs and weather its harsh conditions. ToughStuff products harness the power of the sun and combine high performance, affordability and durability: I have seen Andrew bounce a lamp on the floor without ill effect. In African village huts, rechargeable lamps are gradually replacing the expensive old-fashioned kerosene lamps which are easily knocked over, emit fumes and damage the environment. ToughStuff products enhance connectivity through the use of radios and mobile phones, and create local employment as solar village entrepreneurs sell and hire products through the 'Business in a Box' programme. ToughStuff is contributing to better education: children in East, West and South African countries are now able to study during the evening, often for the first time – no longer suffering damage to eyesight and health that results from trying to study or work with an open flame lamp.

Andrew Tanswell is delighted to be running an enterprise which is helping to lift people out of poverty, improving their quality of life and protecting the environment. He finds powerful motivation in the parable of the talents:

Regardless of the field of expertise we work in, the question is: 'Am I using the skills/expertise/resource/talents he entrusted to me to the best of my ability?' Interestingly, God gave the same words of praise to the two who brought back a return on the resources he gave them. 'Good and faithful servant', he said. When I meet my maker, that's what I hope he will say to me.[28]

4. FROM HOPE TO DESPAIR: EXPLOITATION AND GREED

Many people have difficulty with the Christian doctrine of the fall. They find it difficult to take seriously an ancient story that features a talking serpent and a God walking in the cool of the garden. They may ask why nakedness is shameful: is sin mainly about sex? (Unfortunately, Christians have often given that impression.) They may think God's punishment was out of all proportion to the original man and woman's offence.

But though the story in Genesis 3 presents problems, it also rings a lot of bells. Deep down, we know something is seriously wrong with us. Indeed, theologian Reinhold Niebuhr described original sin as the only empirically verifiable doctrine of the Christian faith.[1] Genesis 3 has power to probe and convict, because it touches on fundamental truths about our human condition.

It is important to ask: what was sinful in Adam and Eve's desire to eat from the tree of the knowledge of good and evil? Genesis 3:5 provides the clue. The key phrase in the serpent's beguiling words is 'you will be like God'. Adam and Eve, who are prototypes of every subsequent human being, rebel against their God-given creaturely status. They seek equality with their creator.

The corporate world provides many examples of human *hubris*. As in other spheres of life, people can be corrupted by power or position; they start to behave with arrogance that brooks no opposition. They aspire to be gods in their own empire. Some chairmen or chief executives pride themselves on the fear they create. Subordinates are cowed into submitting to every whim. 'When he sneezes, we all catch colds' is how one manager I know described his chief executive.

Another feature of the Genesis story that strikes a chord is the way that the culprits pass the buck. Adam blames Eve, and even, by implication, God: 'The woman whom *you* gave to be with me, she gave me fruit from the tree, and I ate' (Genesis 3:12). The woman blames her tempter: 'The serpent tricked me, and I ate' (3:13). It is very difficult to say: 'I'm to blame. I did it, and I'm sorry.'

This is a common tendency in the workplace. Passing the buck is a natural human tendency, reinforced in a corporate climate where admitting mistakes can be either highly detrimental to your career, or leave your company open to expensive legal claims. We seek to shift responsibility, because accepting it seems frighteningly costly. Disowning responsibility is another demonstration of our fallenness.

Regardless of how literally or not we take the details of the Genesis story, the doctrine of the fall tells us that we have missed the mark. We have fallen short of the high calling that God has for us. Human beings deviate from God's purposes for them and his world in an extraordinary variety of ways. God invested such high hopes in this splendid creature made in his image, but the history of the human race must be a grave disappointment to him. In business, as in other areas of life, there is the smell of failure.

Frustration

Work can often be extremely frustrating; the fall affects it in its very essence. The Bible provides vivid pictures of this. In place of the idyllic conditions of the garden of Eden, Genesis 3:17–19 speaks of sweat and toil, thorns and thistles:

> . . . cursed is the ground because of you;
> in toil you shall eat all the days of your life;
> thorns and thistles it shall bring forth for you;
> and you shall eat the plants of the field.
> By the sweat of your face you shall eat bread
> until you return to the ground . . .

Despite advancing technology, it seems impossible to avoid hard grind and some tedious, monotonous routine. Because we are fallen creatures, bearing a punishment for sin, we should not be surprised when work is like this, if it seems to have more than its fair share of difficult and dispiriting moments.

Let's take a brief look at a story you may not have considered in this context. It took place after Jesus' resurrection when the disciples had returned to Galilee. 'Simon Peter said to them [the other disciples], "I am going fishing." They said to him, "We will go with you." They went out and got into the boat, but that night they caught nothing' (John 21:3).

These fishermen were experts. They knew what they were doing when it came to fish. That was why they went out at night: it was the most productive time. They probably had a strong sense of anticipation as they launched their boats that evening; it was the first time they'd been out on the lake for ages. But they fished with a complete lack of success. When morning came, their nets were as empty as when they'd begun. Imagine how they must have felt: tired, frustrated, tetchy, baffled, hungry.

I suspect that their feelings were similar to those of staff at the Prudential, whose 2010 planned takeover of AIA, Asia's arm of America's insurance rival AIG, was stopped at the last minute. This bid reportedly cost Prudential £377m, much of it in lawyers' and accountants' fees.[2] Thousands of hours of work were rendered pointless. One wonders how the staff felt as they came in the next day to start work on a new project. Yet their exasperation may be trifling compared with the despair of staff who work in research laboratories at pharmaceutical companies for seven or eight years on a particular drug, and see this effort come to nothing when trials fail.

What we experience at times like these is the futility of work. A sense of time, money and energy having been wasted: 'a striving after wind . . . What has a man from all the toil and strain with which he toils under the sun?' (Ecclesiastes 2:17, 22). Frustration about work is a prominent theme in Ecclesiastes. Like Peter and his colleagues, we catch nothing, and find it difficult to understand where we've gone wrong. But that is the nature of the world we live in.

Alienation, regimentation and exploitation

Sin impacts the global economy most blatantly in industries that prey on human nature at its weakest and worst. According to one credible estimate, prostitution is a $400 billion global industry, cigarettes bring in $333b, heroin $126b, gambling $110b and pornography $100b.[3] Compared with those figures, worldwide revenues of $10b from human trafficking might seem small, but the lives of sex slaves tend to be bound up in these other repugnant industries as well, making it arguably the most heinous business on earth.

However, pacifists might make that assertion about the armaments industry, which amounted to $1,630b in 2010. The USA is easily the world's biggest spender, with a staggering 42% of world share, six times larger than China, the second on the list. The British BAE Systems has recently overtaken Lockheed Martin and Boeing in the armaments sales table.[4] Even those who don't object to the industry in principle, who believe that military deterrence is a necessity and that war can sometimes be just, may be horrified by the scale of these figures, the considerable illegal trade in arms and the sale of armaments to countries with lamentable human rights records.[5]

Yet human fallenness is equally evident in many organizations which provide goods and services that are innocuous or indeed positively beneficial. The way that work is organized may deform it. The nature of this deformity is summed up in three words that have featured regularly in the social and economic history of the last 250 years: alienation, regimentation and exploitation.

Alienation

Alienation is the separation of things that belong naturally together, antagonism between things or people that belong in harmony. It is a key concept – arguably *the* key concept – in the thinking of Karl Marx. He saw the industrial workers of his day as thoroughly alienated. This is because they had lost control of their own destinies, being under the control of the bourgeoisie, the owners of production, who are concerned with extracting from their labours the maximum amount of surplus value. The effects on the workers, or proletariat, were not simply alienation from the managing classes (producing an 'us and them' mentality), but alienation from their fellow-workers (who are set competitively against each other), their work (which loses meaning because they lack a say in how it is done) and even themselves (they lose touch with their essence as members of the human species).[6]

While we may disagree with Marx's proposed remedies and his prognosis, it is difficult to dispute some truth in his diagnosis. A generation ago, factories in Europe and North America still contained many workers who displayed symptoms of this many-layered form of alienation. Today it is more evident in industrial companies in other parts of the world.

The Bible traces this alienation right back to humanity's original disobedience. Our relationship with God was damaged, and so was our relationship with each other. One serious consequence in Genesis 3 concerns the relationship between the sexes. The fall poisons the relationship of man and woman, particularly in the way he 'rules' over her (Genesis 3:16). In the workplace, this has often resulted in discrimination against women: low pay, lack of promotion and sexual abuse.

The book of Ruth is a charming biblical story with a disquieting undercurrent of sexual harassment. When Ruth the Moabitess bravely decides to work as a gleaner in Bethlehem's barley fields, steps to protect her from molestation by young men are mentioned twice (Ruth 2:9, 22). 'I have ordered the young men not to bother you,' says Boaz. 'It is better, my daughter, that you go out with the young women, otherwise you might be bothered in another field,' says Naomi. It is a sad commentary on the extent of gender alienation, especially the lack of self-control and respect shown by men, that women often have to seek safety in numbers.

Regimentation

Regimentation is rigid organization in the name of control. When work is regimented, what people do and how they do it are governed by strict rules and regulations. It is exemplified by assembly lines that restrict each individual's contribution to performing one particular task. For Marx, it is part of what alienates the worker from their work. But the classic description is by Adam Smith, often thought to be Marx's opposite.

In *The Wealth of Nations*, Smith analyses what he calls 'the very trifling manufacture' of pin making. Whereas one worker making entire pins 'could scarce, perhaps, with his utmost industry, make one pin in a day, and certainly not make twenty', workers divided into eighteen distinct oper-ations – some drawing wire, some fabricating heads, others attaching them, and so forth – 'could increase their individual productivity by 240–4800 per cent'.[7] The division of labour into workers performing specialist functions (some playing to workers' manual skill, others to physical strength) increases efficiency and lowers prices.

But despite Smith's enthusiasm for the overall benefits of the assembly line, he is under no illusions about its negative effect on the workers. Repetitive work deadens the senses: 'The man whose whole life is spent in performing a few simple operations . . . generally becomes as stupid and ignorant as is possible for a human to become.'[8] Significantly, Smith describes the eighteen distinct pin-making operations as performed by 'human hands'. During the nineteenth century industrial workers, especially textile workers in the Lancashire cotton and Yorkshire wool industries, came to be known as *hands*. The implication was that only this part of their body was valued.

Exploitation

Smith also noted how workers are often paid subsistence wages and are especially vulnerable during times of economic recession and stagnation. This brings us to the third aspect, *exploitation*, the use of power in a cruel and unjust manner. Exploitation in business may mean paying workers a pittance, subjecting them to dangerous working conditions, forcing them to work excessively long hours or sacking them without cause. In some countries, there is legal protection against such practices. In many the legal protection is very weak. The scope for exploitation at work is immense.

An issue that arouses increasing indignation is child labour in developing countries. In the Indian states of Tamil Nadu and Andhra Prakesh, for example, thousands of low-caste children as young as nine are bonded into slavery (working to pay off family debts) in order to manufacture *beedis*, a local cigarette. They suffer from high rates of tuberculosis and other lung diseases as a result.[9] Abusive employers often force these children to crouch on the floor for hours in poor light and bad ventilation, breathing in tobacco fumes.

The Bible portrays many situations where workers were exploited. When the immigrant Israelites became a threat to the Egyptian Pharaoh, he decided to 'oppress them with forced labour' (Exodus 1:11). The Egyptian taskmasters made the Israelites' 'lives bitter with hard service in mortar and brick and in every kind of field labour' (1:14). Later it gets worse: in response to Moses' demand to 'let my people go', they are forced to make bricks without being provided with straw (Exodus 5:4–9).

At the height of Israel's power and prosperity, King Solomon employed forced labour in building the temple and palace, which contributed to a rebellion under his son Rehoboam (1 Kings 5:13, 12:3–4, 9–11). The epistle of James berates rich landowners who wouldn't pay the wages of labourers harvesting their fields (James 4:4). In Revelation 18, a vivid picture of the city of Rome under judgment, the cargo whose loss the merchants mourn includes 'slaves, that is, human souls' (Revelation 18:13 ESV). This contains an implicit criticism of the practice of trading in slaves: people should not be bought and sold as chattels.

Working conditions in China: contrasting companies

Alienation, regimentation and exploitation appear to be linked in the disturbing sequence of events at the Chinese company of Foxconn. While on a visit to Hong Kong, I became aware of the extraordinary sequence of suicides (nine, with two further attempts) that took place between March and May 2010 at its Shenzhen plant, just over the border in south-east China. Foxconn is a major manufacturer of electrical components for computers. In particular, it makes iPads, iPods and iPhones for Apple; other notable clients include Hewlett Packard and Dell.

Until recently, 420,000 people worked at the Shenzhen plant, mostly young men and women recruited from rural China. Those who committed suicide were migrant workers aged between seventeen and twenty-five. While they didn't explain why they took their lives (in most cases, by jumping from the building), it is likely that their oppressive working conditions loomed large.

Foxconn employees have lives that are totally dominated by the company, working long hours of overtime and typically sleeping on site with twelve dormitory mates in a small room. Taiwanese ex-army officers act as line supervisors; employees are not allowed to talk and have to ask permission to go to the toilet. They face severe fines for being a minute late; many work standing up all day. It is a distinctly harsh working environment. In response to this spate of suicides, Foxconn has taken various measures, putting nets around the building to catch and deter would-be jumpers, raising wages by 30% and providing 1,000 new psychological counsellors.[10] But the fundamental nature of the work regime appears to be unchanged. The episode raises serious questions, not just for Foxconn but for the American companies and all of us who benefit from the goods that these alienated, regimented and exploited employees churn out so rapidly.

The objection may be made that Foxconn is probably no worse than many similar companies in the Far East and that conditions in European factories were similar at a comparable stage of economic development. That explanation is no excuse. Enlightened employers such as biscuit-maker George Palmer and chocolate manufacturer George Cadbury existed alongside ruthless ones in Victorian England. The same is true in contemporary China. In Hong Kong I had the pleasure of meeting Mr T. S. Wong, Chairman of Jetta Company Ltd. Jetta is one of the best known toy manufacturers in the world, employing close to 40,000 people with production and warehouse space of over 4.5 million square feet in Guangdong, China, and an annual turnover of $400m. Jetta's watchwords are integrity, excellence and synergy. Employees normally work no more than forty hours a week and benefit from libraries, evening classes and open space areas for physical exercise and entertainment. Occupational health and safety are a high priority. T. S. Wong says, 'I always try to treat my employees well, even when other employers would consider that foolish.'

Wong is a Christian whose faith strongly motivates his business conduct. His influence extends well beyond his own company. He is Chairman of the Toy Christian Fellowship (TCF) of Hong Kong, which has over twenty executive members. Unlike many professional fellowships that focus only on evangelism, the TCF seeks to have a wider influence, upholding high standards of safety and fair treatment for workers. When T. S. Wong became the Chairman of Hong Kong Toys Council in 1997 and then President of the International Council of Toy Industries in 2004, he took the opportunity to make this influence count, improving standards for the industry as a whole.[11] That is a powerful form of Christian witness.

The global financial crisis

It is time to examine sins closer to home for those of us in the West. In recent years we have been guilty of greedy and reckless behaviour with serious social repercussions. These are evident in the events that led to the global financial crisis of 2007–9. I shall not attempt a comprehensive analysis of the crisis but suggest that there were six underlying reasons for it.[12]

1. For nearly a decade there was a growing imbalance between different parts of the global economy. Certain countries, such as the USA and the UK, spent and borrowed well beyond their means – relying on other, mainly Asian countries to finance Western debts through their contrasting habits of saving and lending. During the Bush administration the USA's total public debt increased from $5.7 trillion to $10.7 trillion; by February 2012 it had risen to $15.35 trillion. Chinese banks own 26.4% of US treasury bonds and Japanese banks 19.8%.[13]

    Overspending also took place on an individual level. Credit cards are now a symbol of Western society. They were marketed by Access, which subsequently merged with Mastercard, as 'taking the waiting out of wanting': enabling you to have the possessions which money can buy before you have the money to afford them. Use of credit cards rocketed in the UK between 1995 and 2005. Debt owed on credit cards stood at £61b in 2011, roughly equal to half the budget of the National Health Service. Seven per cent of the population are still paying off debts incurred in their Christmas spending six months later.[14]

2. Credit cards, however, are only one form of credit. From the late 1990s to 2007, credit in the West was

increasingly available on easy terms at low rates of interest, notably to home buyers. However, these low rates of interest prompted investors to look for higher returns, accelerating the development of private equity and hedge funds which brought substantial wealth to those in a position to benefit from them. In the UK the directors of these firms earn far more than even the very considerable salaries of senior executives in public limited companies. Two of London's wealthiest hedge fund managers, Noam Gottesman and Pierre Lagrange, founders of GLG Partners, paid themselves an estimated £400m each in 2007.[15] But these new companies used highly sophisticated financial practices, the implications of which were not always fully understood even by those who practised them. The lure of wealth blinded them to risks inherent in their use.

3. Next, there was the packaging, selling and widespread distribution of loans through the process of securitization. This was intended to spread risk, but in sectors where loans were fundamentally unsound (as in the US sub-prime mortgage market) securitization had catastrophic effects when confidence was eroded. In the early 2000s, the Bush administration encouraged mortgage lenders like Government-sponsored Fannie Mae and Freddie Mac to increase their level of loans to low-income Americans and first-time buyers, even though this meant relaxing requirements that borrowers be able to sustain repayments beyond the first two years when interest payments were minimal. Ironically, this was known as an initial 'grace' period. The availability of NINJA loans ('No income, no job, no assets') meant that poor people who were not in a position to buy property were encouraged to borrow

to do so. Meanwhile, banks and financial institutions made substantial profits out of transactions trading their loans. When interest rates went up and the original borrowers defaulted on their payments, the so-called security of these loans proved illusory.

In his perceptive survey of the contemporary world, *What Next?*, former Hong Kong Governor Chris Patten includes this sarcastic anecdote:

> I remember a young banker trying, rather impatiently, to explain to me how the mortgage of an unemployed single parent in St Louis could be morphed into a reliable financial instrument in London, New York or Paris. Impoverishment was magically transformed by clever financial manipulators into a Special Investment Vehicle. The poor got the house, the rich got the bonus. Try as hard as the banker did to get me to comprehend the beautiful simplicities of the whole process, I remained baffled. How stupid of me not to understand what I was being told by this young man, who worked for the Lehman Brothers Bank, RIP.[16]

4. In the banking sector, risky financial strategies were encouraged through excessive focus on short-term results, linked to individual bonus schemes. Banking employees were given strong personal incentives to aim for big returns, ignoring risks not just to their own institution but to the wider economy. The UK Financial Services Authority (FSA), itself criticized for inadequate regulation of the financial sector, has acknowledged that 'inappropriate remuneration policies, practices and procedures were a contributory factor' (though not, it believes, a dominant factor) to the market crisis.

5. Then there was the phenomenon that, in the UK, gave
   the crisis the name 'credit crunch': the rapid switch
   from a pattern of bank lending on very undemanding
   terms to a pattern of banks (for a period) scarcely
   lending at all, due to loss of confidence in the markets.
   I dislike the phrase: it seems to imply that we, the
   public, have an unlimited right to credit, which was
   unfairly curtailed in the wake of the crisis. A measure
   of austerity may have been salutary! Nevertheless, this
   drastic reversal of policy did cause genuine frustration,
   notably for would-be corporate start-ups with sound
   business plans that struggled to access bank loans.

Values and virtues: moderation and prudence

Thus far my analysis tallies with many others that emanate
from secular sources. But another factor has not received the
attention it deserves. Large companies – including the giants
in financial services – frequently proclaimed their allegiance
to moral values, but the depth and rigour of this commitment
is open to question. One leading global investment bank has a
code of ethics that emphasizes the values of honesty and
integrity, but also stipulates that 'From time to time, the firm
may waive certain provisions of its code'.[17] The circumstances
in which this waiver might apply are left unclear. Statements
of corporate values can provide an important rallying-call, but
too often they appear to take second place to the financial
bottom-line. 'Values' is a weak word; it may merely indicate
laudable qualities that companies think are likely (most of the
time) to lead to financial success, not unequivocal commitment
to a way of working regardless of the cost that may accrue.

Christians can make an important contribution here,
because we have a tradition of speaking about *virtues* rather
than values. Virtues are less abstract than values because they

are rooted in persons. A virtue is a good habit, 'a trait of character or intellect which is in some way praiseworthy, admirable or desirable'.[18] The Greek word for 'virtue', *arete*, used in 2 Peter 1:5, means 'moral excellence'. Philosophers and theologians have been thinking and writing about virtues for a long time. Plato identified four *cardinal* virtues: justice, prudence, moderation and courage. In the fourth century AD Ambrose and Augustine put them in a Christian perspective and added three more, the qualities Paul highlights in 1 Corinthians 13 – love, faith and hope – which became known as the *theological* virtues: a total of seven in all. Christians do not necessarily claim that this is a comprehensive list. There are traits that one could add (humility is a prime candidate, in contrast to pride, which the ancient world prized) but most of these can be related to the seven classical virtues or seen as aspects of them.

If we consider the behaviour that led to the financial crisis, two cardinal virtues were notably absent: moderation and prudence. They are the reverse of the vices of greed and folly. Moderation is a word easily misunderstood. It is often associated with mediocrity or a dour lifestyle, marked by abstinence from alcohol, and thought to be the opposite of passion, a quality I have praised in entrepreneurs. But moderation is compatible with passion. It is avoidance of excess, not the opposite of excess. David Runton, founder-owner of the Yorkshire engineering firm FTL, observed at a Faith in Business conference on The Virtues of Business in 2004:

> A moderate gale on the Beaufort scale is pretty windy! It is a journey of risk to any but the skilled sailor. Moderation may be only one stage away from excess – it can be that close – but the skilled practitioner knows when to exercise self-control and contain himself.[19]

Prudence too is an often misunderstood virtue, being wrongly equated with caution. As James Allcock, a former senior executive with British Gas, said at the same conference, undue caution will wreck a business. Business leaders can rarely afford to do nothing: it is often true that any action is better than no action. There is a time for seizing opportunities and taking risks, especially in starting a business. But wise businesspeople take carefully calculated risks, so that the company survives if a strategy or policy fails. Prudence steers a businessperson between undue risk and paralysing caution.[20]

What is prudence? James Allcock favoured C. S. Lewis' definition: practical common sense, taking the trouble to think out what you are doing and what is likely to come of it. So it is prudent to tell the truth at meetings with analysts and shareholders. They don't like being given nasty shocks when the profits turn out to be much smaller than expected.

In the early 2000s, moderation and prudence were lacking in the behaviour of that once prudent, respectable building society from north-east England, Northern Rock. After it metamorphosed into a bank in 1997, it chose to become extremely competitive in segments of the mortgage market, yet refused to accept the constraint of its small base of customer deposits. Instead, under its flamboyant Chief Executive, Adam Applegarth, Northern Rock borrowed billions from other banks on the international money markets. It offered mortgages where the loan represented the full value of the property and borrowers were allowed to certify their own incomes – an invitation to exaggerate their incomes to qualify for a larger loan. This was a repetition of the NINJA phenomenon in the US sub-prime market. When the property boom declined, both in the US and the UK, Northern Rock was extremely vulnerable. Other banks stopped lending it money. Applegarth had only one strategy for growth and no contingency plan. There was a 'run on the bank' in September 2007 as people queued to remove their deposits. It was saved only by Government intervention: first in guaranteeing the security of all remaining deposits, and then in nationalizing the bank. Applegarth had to resign.

Financial analyst Peter Warburton has suggested that events at Northern Rock underline the truth of Proverbs 22:

- 'A good name is more desirable than great riches; to be esteemed is better than silver or gold' (22:1).
- 'A prudent man sees danger and takes refuge, but the simple keep going and suffer for it' (22:3).
- 'The rich rule over the poor and the borrower is servant to the lender' (22:7).[21]

In business, arrogance is a sure recipe for imprudence, and imprudence is a sure recipe for disaster.

Oracles against Tyre: pride before a fall

The neglect of the Christian virtues is symptomatic of Europe's abandonment of the moral and spiritual bedrock on which it built its greatness. In this situation I suggest there is no more relevant portion of Scripture to heed than Ezekiel's oracles against the sea-port Tyre.

Tyre was a city that punched above its weight on the ancient Middle Eastern scene. This was largely due to its two excellent harbours, one on the mainland and the other on an offshore island, connected by a causeway that doubled the city's trading potential. It was famous for glassware and dyed cloth, using purple and scarlet dye made from local shellfish. Yet Tyre was a small country, vulnerable to interference from the major powers of Middle Eastern politics. In the seventh century BC it came under Assyrian sway, but retained partial autonomy by paying a large tribute. From about 630, Assyria was in decline, and for the next forty-five years, Tyre's sea-trade flourished; but the next major empire, Babylon, was looming on the horizon. At this historical juncture, Ezekiel devotes three chapters of prophecy to Tyre. Each takes a different tack, though they have connecting links. They were probably written in 586, just after Jerusalem had fallen to the Babylonians.

In chapter 26, God pronounces judgment on Tyre because it has rejoiced over the downfall of Jerusalem, saying, 'Aha, broken is the gateway of the peoples' (Ezekiel 26:2). 'Gateway' suggests a meeting point of international trade routes where tolls were exacted. Tyre is gloating at the loss of a commercial competitor. Even though Jerusalem's fall lay within God's purpose, as a punishment for the sins of the Jewish people, others should not take pleasure in such things. Tyre's punishment is that it will become a bare rock (26:4, 14), a clear play on its name, which means 'rock' – fit for nothing but fishermen spreading out their nets to dry.

In chapter 27, the prophet tells the story of Tyre's downfall in a contrasting way. This is a *lamentation* (27:2), not a proclamation, even including the unusual literary device of a lament within a lament (27:32). In an inspired feat of poetic imagination, Ezekiel pictures Tyre as a magnificent ship, superbly fitted out and expertly crewed, with with timbers, mast and oars made from wood of the highest quality, and sail and awnings of fine linen. He mentions sixteen different places that these materials and men came from. Keel of fir planks from Hermon, mast of cedar of Lebanon, oars of oak from Bashan . . . so it goes on. Rowers, pilots, caulkers and mercenary soldiers all get a mention. Each made a contribution: 'they gave you splendour' (27:10); 'they made perfect your beauty' (27:11).

Next Ezekiel catalogues the countries that Tyre traded with and the products in which she traded (27:12–25). Twenty-six are named, systematically arranged from Tarshish in the west up to Damascus in the north and on to exotic Arabian place-names in the east. Forty items of merchandise are mentioned, a fascinating selection, including fine linen, ivory tusks, white wool, wrought iron, sweet cane, precious stones and magnificent carpets. All this agrees with what we know of Tyre's trading exploits from other sources.

Ezekiel provides this plethora of detail to build up an impression of formidable power. We are confronted by a city that is highly self-confident, a confidence borne of affluence, commercial skill and use of the most advanced current technology. Tyre was no mean city.

However, the irony is that the fine ship Tyre is so laden with goods that in heavy seas and a fierce east wind it sinks to the bottom of the ocean (Ezekiel 27:25–27). Tyre's downfall takes place 'in the heart of the seas' – a phrase that recurs three times (27:25, 26, 27) – the very place where it felt secure and supreme. Its fall inspires lament: the mariners and pilots 'stand on the shore and wail aloud over you' (27:29–30). As in chapter 26, mourning is intense and prolonged.

It is striking how the seafarers give credit to Tyre's achievements. 'When your wares came from the seas you satisfied many peoples; with your abundant wealth and merchandise you enriched the kings of the earth' (27:33). Tyre had created wealth for others as well as itself. There is no explicit criticism of Tyre in Ezekiel 27. For the prophet, this is astonishingly neutral reporting. But verse 3 contains a hint of God's perspective, though this too appears to be spoken in sorrow rather than anger: 'Thus says the Lord God: O Tyre, you have said, "I am perfect in beauty"' (Ezekiel 27:3) Tyre had a high opinion of itself. Was that the seed of its downfall?

Chapter 28 answers: yes. Here the prophet returns to judgment mode. It is precisely because Tyre's heart is proud and said 'I am a god' that the real God is bringing enemies against it. Even here, however, we feel a sense of regret. Tyre did have an impressive record of achievement: 'by your wisdom and understanding you have amassed wealth for yourself, and have gathered gold and silver into your treasures. By your great wisdom in trade you have increased your wealth . . . ' (28:4–5). Tyre may have been blessed with a fine natural situation, but it had made the most of it, showing initiative and ingenuity. Nevertheless, Tyre is sternly reminded twice: 'You are but a mortal, and no god' (28:2, 9).

In Ezekiel 28:11–19, the story of the fall is retold in an unexpected way. The king of Tyre is pictured as the epitome of perfect primeval man, in the garden of Eden, or 'holy mountain of God' (28:13–14). He is dressed in ten magnificent precious stones – an allusion to Tyre's prosperity. The king or prince of Tyre at the time was Itobaal II, but the criticism feels less a personal attack on him than a comment on the ethos of Tyre itself. This oracle is a fresh take on Genesis 1–3. Ezekiel highlights *both* the perfection of God's human creation – 'You were the signet of perfection, full of wisdom and perfect in beauty' (28:12); 'you were blameless in your ways, from the day you were created' (28:15) – *and* the headlong nature of man's fall – 'I cast you as a profane thing from the mountain of God' (28:16); 'I cast you to the ground' (28:17). The message is clear. It is precisely the greatness of Tyre's status that serves to accentuate the tragedy of its fall.

The main problem, as we have seen, was Tyre's self-congratulatory pride. But Ezekiel now critiques Tyre's trading practice. 'In the abundance of your trade you were filled with violence and you sinned' (28:16); 'in the unrighteousness of your trade, you profaned your sanctuaries' (28:18). Here we would like to know more. In what way was Tyre filled with violence, and its trade unrighteous? Was one objectionable feature the way that it traded in human beings, as indicated by 27:13: 'they exchanged human beings and vessels of bronze for your merchandise'?[22] Did the power of its position lead it to bully and threaten trading partners? That is a common consequence of pride.

Is all this of merely historical interest? No. Ezekiel's oracles against Tyre can help the countries of the West to arrive at a properly nuanced understanding of our situation. As chapter 2 showed, we live amidst polarized views, with some in the West blithely complacent about global capitalism and others fiercely critical. In the words of Harvard historian David Landes, some see the European dominance of the last 500 years as 'the triumph of good over bad. The Europeans, they say, were smarter, better organised, harder working. The others were ignorant, arrogant, lazy, backward, superstitious'. Others see it as a triumph of bad over good. 'The Europeans, they say, were aggressive, ruthless, greedy, unscrupulous, hypocritical; their victims were happy, innocent, weak – waiting victims and hence thoroughly victimised.'[23]

I believe there are elements of truth in both views. The West deserves some credit for its wealth creation. In particular, it has generated wealth partly through commendable *cultural* habits – for example, a disciplined work ethic, integrity in public service, and a capacity for innovation and enterprise. National cultures score differently on these criteria. But here's the rub: sixth-century Tyre could probably have claimed the same. They too displayed industriousness and ingenuity. Yet the fact that much in Tyre's achievements and in the West's is good should not blind us to what is bad and unjust. The West has also generated wealth for itself through treating the 'Rest'[24] unfairly – through bullying, slavery and exploitation.

We too fall under the judgment of God. We are exposed to his searching gaze.

The tragedy is that many people in the countries whose collective faith inspired their economic ascent no longer acknowledge this God at all. I shared these thoughts from Ezekiel at a Faith and Business conference in Uppsala, attended by twenty-five businessmen from Sweden and Norway. They could see the relevance of these chapters to their situation, as I can to the UK. Sweden and Norway are admirable countries in many ways. Free of the scourge of corruption, they are populated by hard-working people with a strong egalitarian commitment to reducing the disparities of wealth.[25] Having experienced their own banking crisis in the early 1990s, they learnt from their mistakes and have come through the global financial crisis relatively untroubled, sensibly steering clear of the Eurozone. Yet these countries with a strong Lutheran heritage have largely abandoned it; very few Swedes and Norwegians go to church. Secularization is accelerating fast. The danger is that they, like us, become complacent and take pride in their own efforts. I am not suggesting that Stockholm, Oslo or London are about to slide under the sea in judgment. But I do believe we forsake our forefathers' faith at our peril, and that unpleasant surprises are likely for people who become 'wise in their own eyes' (Isaiah 5:21).

Responding to earthquakes: cooperatives in Chile

A major issue which Christians often associate with the fall is the phenomenon of natural disaster: the periodic eruption of earthquakes, volcanoes, hurricanes and floods, which cause incalculable suffering to the human and animal creation. Theologians acknowledge the presence of mystery, and vary in their understanding of the causal connections, but most feel that the world shows clear signs of 'bondage to decay' (Romans 8:21) because it is fallen. Here I shall highlight the impact of natural disasters on business.

Chile suffers an exceptional number of earthquakes. This long, thin country runs parallel to the fault line known as the Atacama Trench, 5,900 kilometres long and 180 kilometres off the South American coast. Chile experiences minor tremors on a regular basis but every twenty or twenty-five years is subject to an earthquake of massive proportions. In 1939 it was Chillán, with an estimated 30,000 killed; in 1960 the most powerful earthquake ever recorded (9.5 on the Richter scale) hit the southern city of Valdivia; in 1985 it was the turn of the capital, Santiago; and most recently the earthquake of 27 February 2010 struck the seaport city of Concepcion, its devastating impact extending far across Chile's Central Valley.

On a recent visit to Chile to meet fair trade producers, I witnessed the effects of the 2010 earthquake and discussed what it was like living in a country so vulnerable to seismic activity. Compared to many other countries in the world today, Chile is strongly Christian: about 60% of its population are practising Catholics and 15% practising Protestants. In churches and cathedrals I saw clear evidence of the depth of this piety: people on their knees praying with real fervour.

Among many friendly, helpful Chileans that I met, Chino Henríquez, the Managing Director of Apicoop, a large honey producers' cooperative, was especially engaging. As we drove through the streets of Valdivia I asked him if the frequency and severity of earthquakes caused Chileans to question belief in God. His answer was no, he thought not: it was more likely they would pray to God for help. In addition, Chileans have both a philosophical and a resourceful attitude, accepting that they live in an area where earthquakes happen on a regular basis, taking sensible precautionary measures, fleeing to higher ground in the hour's time-lapse between an earthquake and the tsunami which follows, and building houses with increasingly strong materials. As a result, the loss of human life in Chilean earthquakes of recent years has been relatively small.

However, in any disaster, some are unlucky. In the central town of Curico, at the heart of Chile's burgeoning wine-growing area, I visited Lautaro Wines, a wine producers' cooperative with twenty-two members. Four farmers lost their houses in the 2010 earthquake, with seven other homes being seriously damaged; some have now been rebuilt and improved. One man, José, lost eight relatives including his wife and two of his children; I spoke to him in the café run by his one surviving daughter. He himself was dragged from the wreckage of his home three hours after the earthquake. Oddly, even more shocking than the carnage of ruined buildings was the damage caused to the vats where the wine is stored. These are huge steel containers and look impregnable, but the tremor battered, twisted and mangled many to a point where they were unusable and the wine lost. Irrigation systems were also badly damaged. The earthquake happened at the worst possible time, in the middle of the harvesting season; Lautaro Wines lost $200,000 in wine they already had in stock.

In the face of this suffering (which we will never fully understand), the solidarity shown by the wine producers was truly impressive. The value of belonging to a cooperative was evident. Members rallied round those most severely affected, especially José. Grants had been made available for funeral expenses, medical care and the rebuilding of houses. Two of Lautaro's European fair trade partners, the UK organization Traidcraft and Oxfam Belgium, made significant financial contributions. The wine producers have been through a sobering and chastening experience, but I found them in surprisingly buoyant spirits. With a good harvest in 2011, they got the business back on track.[26] My experience with Lautaro and Apicoop was that I saw producers' cooperatives working more effectively in Chile than in other parts of the world I have visited. I found myself thinking that their capacity for human solidarity – for working together rather than operating individualistically – is probably borne out of a shared experience of suffering: surviving and resisting the Pinochet regime, and the recurrent earthquakes.

Suffering of an extreme kind can provoke the worst in human behaviour (like the looting and pillaging that follow some disasters) and therefore lead to despair. But shared suffering can also bring out the best in people, and give rise to hope. This is also true of the suffering discussed earlier in the chapter, pain which is more directly attributable to human sin: alienation, regimentation and exploitation, along with the vices of greed and folly. Cruel injustice can provoke heroic resistance; appalling blunders may give way to sober resolve.

Hope and suffering are not necessarily in contradiction. The passage in which Paul talks about the earth being in bondage to decay is profoundly hopeful: the word 'hope' occurs six times. The creation's bondage lies within the overall purpose of God and will not last indefinitely. We shall return to this theme in chapter 9, but in the meantime, after a chapter devoted to the effects of the fall, let us draw hope from the apostle's words:

> For the creation waits with eager longing for the revealing of the children of God; for the creation was subjected to futility, not of its own will but by the will of the one who subjected it, in hope that the creation itself will be set free from the

bondage to decay and will obtain the freedom of the glory of the children of God... For in hope we were saved. Now hope that is seen is not hope. For who hopes for what is seen? But if we hope for what we do not see, we wait for it with patience. (Romans 8:19–21, 24–25)

5. HOPE FOR A NATION: NO DEBT, NO CORRUPTION

The stark reality of the fall confronted God with a choice. Should he persist with this project in which he had invested so much hope in human beings? There are moments in Genesis 4–11 when God appears to be on the verge of losing hope and abandoning the project.

> The Lord saw that the wickedness of humankind was great in the earth, and that every inclination of the thoughts of their hearts was only evil continually. And the Lord was sorry that he had made humankind on the earth, and it grieved him to his heart.
> (Genesis 6:5–6)

God came close to wiping out the human race. Even after Noah survives, and God's subsequent covenant that 'never again shall all flesh be cut off by the waters of a flood' (Genesis 9:11), a further outbreak of human self-aggrandizement fuels God's anger. This time it is a corporate act, the building of the tower of Babel, prompted by people wanting to 'make a name' for themselves; it provokes the divine judgment of scattering humanity over the face of the earth (Genesis 11:4, 8). As Old Testament scholar Christopher Wright comments, 'The effects of sin have now reached "global" proportions. What can God do next?'[1]

The answer is that God focuses his attention on one individual, Abraham, and the nation that will be descended from him. God will make himself known in a special, unmistakeable way to a particular people as a loving, powerful and holy

God. He reveals himself to the Hebrew patriarchs, rescues their great-grandchildren from Egyptian oppression, gives them a land to inhabit and makes his design for life known to them in copious detail by providing the law. God's relationship with the Jewish people is unique. They were a specially chosen people, as the prophets proclaimed: 'When Israel was a child I loved him, and out of Egypt I called my son' (Hosea 11:1); 'you only have I known of all the families of the earth' (Amos 3:1). Indeed, there are times when Israel's God looks like a tribal God, bringing them victory in wars with other nations. It feels like God has written off the rest of the human race – so wary should the Israelites be about moral contamination by them. But that is not the whole story. God is still passionately concerned for the whole of his creation.

Thus right from the start of this new, third act in the drama, God promises Abraham not only that 'I will make of you a great nation, and I will bless you', but that 'in you all the families of the earth shall be blessed' (Genesis 12:2–3). This is repeated even when God announces judgment against the wicked cities of Sodom and Gomorrah; the implication is that through keeping 'the way of the Lord by doing righteousness and justice', Abraham and his descendants will be 'a blessing to the nations' (Genesis 18:18–19). Before entering the Promised Land, the Israelites are urged to observe God's laws diligently, not just for their own benefit, but because of the impression made upon the nations (Deuteronomy 4:6). Even when the Jews, because of their failings, have gone into exile, God's purpose is still that they serve as a 'light to the nations' (Isaiah 42:6, 49:6). Psalm 67 is a prayer that God may 'be gracious to us and bless us' so that 'your way may be known upon earth, your saving power among all nations'. The aim is that 'all the peoples' will praise God

(Psalm 67:1–3). So in concentrating upon a particular nation, God is looking for some positive knock-on effects. Wright observes that God's purpose was 'to create a new community of people who in their social life would embody those qualities of righteousness, peace, justice and love that reflect God's own character and were God's original purpose for humanity'.[2]

Working as God intended

This model pattern of behaviour included God's will for the economic sphere. We have noted several Old Testament passages that show people cultivating land and trading products and skills. Some of these descriptions have an 'ideal' character; we see individuals and groups working as God meant them to work. Here are two examples.

Proverbs 31:10–31

This final section of Proverbs is a paean to the 'capable wife' or 'virtuous woman'. The main focus is on her economic productivity. Through her business acumen she serves her family and extended household. She is praised for:

- technical skill and manual dexterity: 'She puts her hand to the distaff, and her hands hold the spindle' (31:19)
- trading with the wider community: 'She makes linen garments and sells them; she supplies the merchant with sashes' (31:24)
- indefatigable hard work and ability to delegate: 'She rises while it is still night and provides food for her household and tasks for her servant-girls' (31:15)
- wisdom in investment decisions and agriculture: 'She considers a field and buys it; with the fruit of her hands she plants a vineyard' (31:16)

- physical and mental strength, giving her confidence for the future: 'Strength and dignity are her clothing, and she laughs at the time to come' (31:25)
- clothing her family and equipping her house: 'She is not afraid for her household when it snows, for all her household are clothed in crimson' (31:21; crimson refers to dyed wool, but a similar Hebrew word, 'double-clothed' for extra warmth, may be more accurate).[3]
- generosity in the community: 'She opens her hand to the poor, and reaches out her hands to the needy' (31:20).

No wonder that this woman's husband praises her: ' "Many women have done excellently, but you surpass them all.' Charm is deceitful, and beauty is vain, but a woman who fears the Lord is to be praised' (31:29–30).

Interestingly, this impressive woman who combines business virtuosity with family commitment seems to inspire black Christian women particularly, both in African-American communities in the USA and the developing world. There are frequent references to Proverbs 31 in networks like Sisters in Business[4] and the Enterprising Business Woman Institute for Entrepreneurial Learning.[5] This reflects the increasingly prominent role women play in the small business sector of the global economy, despite their underrepresentation in large corporations. The overwhelming majority of loans – world-wide 75% – made by micro-finance organizations go to women, most running micro-enterprises from home.[6] This is because women are much less likely to waste the loans than men; they are better at providing moral support for each other in groups of loanees; and their repayment rates are higher.

While the virtuous woman of Proverbs 31 seems to be more prosperous and privileged than most of the recipients of these loans (her husband was 'known in the city gate, taking his seat among the elders of the land', 31:23), the home-based business that she ran bears similarities to theirs. It is not surprising that inspires their attempts to climb out of poverty.

2 Kings 12:9–19

This describes the repair of the Jerusalem temple during the reign of Jehoash. It takes place belatedly; the king reprimands the priests for doing nothing with money donated several years previously. But once they have been stung into proceeding, the repairs run smoothly. Notable features include:

- a system for handling money: donations put into the treasure chest were passed on by the king's secretary and the high priest to the overseers as the money became available and when it was needed; the overseers (main contractors) bought the materials and paid the sub-contractors (12:9–12).
- an operation that draws on many talents, including carpenters, builders, masons and stonecutters – all employing specialist skills (12:11–12).
- a right ordering of priorities: this was restoration, not embellishment. Money was paid to the workers, not spent on fancy additions – 'for the house of the Lord no basins of silver, snuffers, bowls, trumpets, or any vessels of gold, or of silver, were made' (12:13–14).
- an impeccable reputation for honesty: the overseers are considered so trustworthy that they are not required to account for their handling of the money given to them, 'for they dealt honestly' (12:15).

The narrator of 2 Kings does not make a fuss of this episode, which makes it additionally impressive. Almost incidentally he paints a picture of a well-run building project, a snapshot of a trustworthy construction industry. In the contemporary world, construction is a sector that bristles with challenges. It is a very fragmented industry, which involves coordinating the activities of many different types of worker. In the UK, there has been a gradual shift from an adversarial style of buyer-supplier relationship to a more collaborative approach, the hallmark of which is partnership, but progress has been patchy.[7] Trust is hard won and easily lost. It would only have needed one dishonest supervisor, pocketing some of the money or unfairly distributing rewards and resources to stone-masons, to jeopardize the repair of the Jerusalem temple.

Interpreting the Old Testament Law

Any consideration of economics in the Old Testament cannot avoid the wealth of material in the books of the Law. Of the 613 specific commandments, about a sixth relate to the economic sphere. These cover: business practices; treatment of employees, servants and slaves; injuries and damages; property and property rights; the sabbatical and jubilee years; agriculture and animal husbandry; times and seasons.[8] Some of these topics are treated discretely, others in a seemingly random way, cheek by jowl with laws concerning very different areas of life.

Leviticus 19 exemplifies this. It raises challenging issues about the use we should make of the Old Testament law in the present world. On the one hand, some commands feel very familiar. Most of the ten commandments are included – for example, do not make idols, do not steal, do not witness falsely (Leviticus 19:4, 11). Their continuing relevance is obvious, and is reinforced in the New Testament. Leviticus 19:18 says 'love your neighbour as yourself', which Jesus picked from relative obscurity to affirm as one of the two great commandments, alongside the command to 'love the

Lord your God' (Mark 12:29–31). On the other hand, the chapter includes rulings about men sleeping with slave-girls (19:20) or trimming beards (19:27) where the reason for the law is not easily understood. In some ways Leviticus 19 speaks across and stands above different cultures; in others it seems locked into a particular culture.

It is possible to go through this chapter systematically distinguishing between the two – arguing that certain laws remain valid now while others no longer apply.[9] But even when a law seems strange, it's worth exploring to identify the fundamental principle at stake. This is not always straightforward, but with careful exegesis and knowledge of the historical context, progress is possible. It's then well worth trying to reapply that principle, with some imagination and effort, to our own culture. This is the approach taken by Christopher Wright. He distinguishes his position from two polar opposites, commonly found across global Christianity. The first is to seek to replicate Israelite society now by heavy, literal adherence to Old Testament laws.

> Such literal imitation is not only practically impossible (because we do not live in the world of an ancient Near Eastern agrarian economy and tribal culture); it is also theologically impossible (because neither the church nor any modern state stands in exactly the same relationship to God as Israel did in the Old Testament).[10]

The second is to dismiss the law as irrelevant, on the grounds that it has been fulfilled in Christ, replaced by grace, or relegated to a past dispensation. Wright comments:

> All such neglect of the Old Testament for ethical purposes seems to me impossible to reconcile with either the seal of

Jesus' authority on the abiding validity of the law and the prophets (Matthew 5:17–20), or Paul's affirmation that all Scripture (meaning the Old Testament) is not only inspired but also profitable for ethical guidance and written for our instruction (2 Timothy 3:16–17; 1 Corinthians 10:1–13).[11]

The intermediate way that Wright commends is to regard the society and laws of Israel as *paradigms*. This is 'a model or pattern that enables you to explain or critique many different and varying situations by means of some single concept or set of governing principles'.[12] We should pay attention to both the particularity of the original law and the universality pertaining to the principle we can derive from it. A similar approach, using 'analogy' rather than 'paradigm', is found in ethicist William Spohn's *Go and Do Likewise*: 'Analogy illuminates what was hidden before and pulls the past into the present. As Mark Twain said, history doesn't repeat itself, but it does rhyme. The work of analogical imagination is to catch that rhyme.'[13]

With this approach in mind, let's consider the gleaning command in Leviticus 19:9–10:

> When you reap the harvest of your land, you shall not reap to the very edges of your field, or gather the gleanings of your harvest. You shall not strip your vineyard bare, or gather the fallen grapes of your vineyard; you shall leave them for the poor and alien.

The law with its rationale is repeated in Leviticus 23:22. In ancient Israel most people possessed their plot of land, but some had lost it through indolence, misfortune or oppression. God says clearly that these people are not to be abandoned. The first principle we can 'glean' from this law is that society should provide adequately for their welfare. Landowners should not be obsessed with garnering every last bit of produce from their field. In the divine economy there is room for good stewardship, but also for reckless generosity: an attitude rooted in the knowledge that God is generous and the land ultimately belongs to God.

Notice that allowing gleaning is not distributing handouts. The poor had to work for what they got. They picked up the leftover grain from the edges of the fields. When Ruth gleaned behind the reapers, she was on her feet from early in the morning until the evening, and then beat the pickings into an ephah of barley (Ruth 2:7, 17). This helped the poor keep their dignity; they were not spongers. So preservation of dignity is the second principle implicit in this law. It is an ancient example of the work-for-welfare principle: work and welfare going hand in hand. This is a topical issue in the UK, and while there is certainly scope for debate about its application, the principle is both sound and biblical.

The prohibition on interest

Among the various texts in the Torah relating to economic issues, one topic is particularly controversial: the charging of interest. It is an issue on which the churches have, over the centuries, changed their position, prohibition turning to permission. Not all Christians are convinced that this shift was justified, however. In the light of debt-related financial problems, highlighted by the global crisis, some critics have become more vocal then ever.

Three key passages in the Torah prohibit the charging of interest.

Exodus 22:25–27 occurs in a section with a profoundly covenantal feel: God expresses concern to his people on matters about which he cares passionately. It consists of laws protecting disenfranchised and vulnerable groups, including widows, orphans, resident non-Israelites ('aliens') and the poor, people struggling for 'basic economic subsistence'.[14] Concern for the poor leads to the stipulation that interest should not be charged on loans to them. These loans, and the compassionate handling of essential items that were pawned, were meant to help people cope with extreme poverty; lenders should not see them as a source of gain.

Care and respect for the poor are rooted in the drama of salvation history. In the words of commentator T. E. Fretheim, 'When the people of God mistreat the poor, they violate their own history. . . . it is a disavowal of their own past, of those salvific acts which made them what they were.'[15]

Leviticus 25:35–38 envisages a situation where a fellow countryman has fallen on hard times and is dependent on others. The call is to be supportive and compassionate, treating such people with the kindness shown to resident aliens. Solidarity is expressed by not charging interest. This prohibition is supported by a basic premise of biblical faith, the fear of God. Again the people are reminded of God's mercy as a ground for showing mercy themselves.

Deuteronomy 23:19–20 breaks new ground. It explicitly forbids the charging of interest within the Israelite community while permitting interest on loans to foreigners. Here the prohibition is not confined to poor Israelites, and obedience is linked to God's blessing. The close-knit community ties that lie at the heart of the prohibition are highlighted by the permission to treat foreigners differently. Wright notes that this was not the stranger living in their midst, but the stranger who lived in a foreign nation, with whom there was no land-kinship network.[16] In that context, levying interest on loans was a sensible minimization of risk, and meant that Israel could take its place as an equal partner in the commercial arena of the ancient Middle East, where charging interest was normal.

Other Old Testament texts mention interest more briefly, but always with disapproval. In Psalm 15 the righteous person who may dwell in God's sanctuary is one who, among other things, lends his money without interest (15:5). The righteous man of Ezekiel 18:8, 13 and 17 is similarly restrained. Nehemiah becomes furious when, in a post-exilic urban context, he learns of Israelites exacting interest from fellow-countrymen and forcing them into slavery (Nehemiah 5:1–12). Do not underestimate the strength of feeling in these texts.

Church tradition and usury

It was on the basis of these Old Testament prohibitions that the early Church Fathers condemned taking interest. They believed that it broke the law of charity and set the ban within the broader context of teaching which required the sharing of wealth. Cyprian of Carthage and Gregory of Nyssa both deplored the deceit of the lender, who appears to be a friend to the borrower but is in fact an enemy. Gregory also argued that lending at interest is a sin unknown to nature because it draws gain from inanimate things, whereas in nature only living things provide fruit.[17] This resembles Aristotle's idea that money is intrinsically sterile.

As the Church moved into the medieval period, the word 'usury' (derived from the Latin *usura*) was applied to the charging of interest. Although this now tends to be used of exorbitant interest, it originally applied to any interest. The great Church councils took a consistently negative view of the practice. The Council of Nicaea (325) ordered usurious clergy to be deposed; the Council of Carthage (345) condemned its practice by laity; the third Lateran Council (1179) denied usurers the sacrament or Christian burial; and the second Council of Lyons (1274) forbade the letting of property to foreign usurers.

Medieval Christians mostly retained earlier arguments for condemning usury. Peter Lombard claimed that usury 'is contained under robbery',[18] the seventh commandment. Among the Scholastic theologians, this equation between usury and robbery became common. They anticipated the counterargument that the borrower had agreed to the transaction by saying that he did so with a forced will rather than a voluntary will.[19]

Thomas Aquinas' teaching on usury was highly influential. He followed Aristotle in the belief that money was essentially barren, so it was 'unnatural' to make money out of money. Money is a means of exchange, and to lend it at interest is to sell what does not exist. He regards this as a matter of justice: 'Making a charge for lending money is unjust in itself, for one party sells the other something non-existent, and this . . . sets up an inequality which is contrary to justice.'[20] Aquinas broadens the Old Testament stipulations to include even the foreigner. Christians 'ought to treat every man as a brother and neighbour, especially in the epoch of the Gospel'.[21]

Ironically, the medieval era saw Jewish people emerge as the major moneylenders of Europe. Because Deuteronomy 23 allowed them to lend to foreigners (as they considered Gentiles to be), along with the fact that they were barred from many other forms of commerce, Jews became notorious as usurers. Christians often reviled them for charging interest, but that did not stop them borrowing from Jews when they needed a loan. Shakespeare's play *The Merchant of Venice* reveals the connection between economics and anti-Semitism.

Aquinas has much to say about the relational aspects of lending and borrowing. A person who pays interest on a loan 'cannot be said to be acting quite voluntarily, but under some pressure'.[22] Therefore, a 'debt of gratitude is set up'—the borrower is under 'a moral obligation'.[23] Interestingly, Aquinas goes on to say that this means the lender is entitled to some compensation and, if he does not charge interest, that compensation should be benevolence towards the lender.[24]

This switch of perspective is significant. It raises the possibility that, just as a loan with interest can entail a lender taking advantage of a borrower, a loan without interest can entail a borrower taking advantage of a lender. If the lender stands to lose by the loan, is it unjust that he receives financial compensation? From the early thirteenth century, certain Scholastic theologians argued that a creditor could sometimes claim compensation for loss suffered because of failure on the borrower's part to repay the loan on time. Norwegian scholar Odd Langholm explains:

> From such loss because of delay, the basis of the claim for compensation was extended to a creditor's loss on account of the loan within the loan period itself, and the concept of a loss was extended from a loss actually sustained (*damnum emergens*) to a loss in the relative sense of a missed profit opportunity (*lucrum cessans*).[25]

Where these two exceptions were allowed, a major crack in the church's traditional teaching opened up. By the sixteenth century, such exceptions had become commonplace in the thinking of the influential Spaniards Luis de Molina and Juan de Lugo. This was a decisive break with the earlier tradition.

The Reformation watershed

In the meantime the world was changing fast – socially, economically and politically. Developing economies and the growth of a new merchant middle class were making it difficult to carry on transactions without taking interest. The two great Reformers, Martin Luther and John Calvin, held rather different views on the subject of usury.

Luther stands solidly in the Scholastic tradition. He uses a variety of arguments against the practice in his famous treatise *On Trade and Usury*. He states that it is 'simply a commandment that we are bound to obey',[26] and sees the widespread practice of usury as part of the perilous end-time in which he believed he was living. With typically colourful language, Luther says that usury 'lays burdens upon all lands, cities, lords and people, sucks them dry and brings them to ruin'.[27] He presents an alternative – generous, open-handed giving or lending. Moreover, usurers who charge a high rate 'often die an unnatural death or come to some terrible end . . . for God is a judge for the poor and needy'.[28] Luther's main target in attacking usury was what he saw as the greedy merchant-class.

Calvin lived in the merchant city of Geneva and had a less jaundiced view of their practices. In a letter to Claude de Sachin, he offers cautious advice on the subject of charging interest.[29] He argues that usury almost always travels with two inseparable companions: tyrannical cruelty and the art of deception.

Nevertheless, he saw the Israelite ban on usury as temporary, an aspect of their constitution appropriate to their time and place. Sixteenth-century Geneva was different: it was a political union whereas Old Testament Israel was a fraternal one. He concludes that 'we ought not to judge usury according to a few passages of scripture, but in accordance with the principle of equity',[30] therefore thinking it permissible 'to make concessions to the common utility'.[31] He considered that loans at modest rates between parties with good business reasons to lend and borrow were acceptable.[32] However, Calvin is clear that no-one should take interest from the poor. The lender must not be preoccupied by personal gain; otherwise he forgets the bonds of relationship and ties of community.

Significantly, Calvin did not use the Aristotle-Aquinas argument about the barrenness of money. During the sixteenth century, there was an increasing abandonment of this argument and a growing acceptance that money, too, was a commodity. So money had its price, and interest named the price it carried for the privilege of borrowing it over a period of time. As commerce developed, so did the need for long-term investment: the outlay of costs might be consider-able before any profits could be anticipated. Entrepreneurs needed loans to get started, and the bankers providing them could justifiably expect some return for their services.

Charging interest is also difficult to avoid when inflation is a fact of life. If lenders' money will be worth less when returned, it seems fair for them to charge interest, as well as if they carry a significant risk of losing it.

This changed view of money makes the sixteenth century a crucial watershed in the Church's tradition on usury. In accepting modest rates of interest, post-Reformation theo-logians weren't rejecting all the principles of the preceding tradition. Calvin and others correctly discerned that the main principle behind the biblical prohibitions was protection of the poor, a zealous concern that they should not be exploited in their vulnerable condition. But they no longer felt that this necessitated a blanket ban on all interest. Effectively they exhorted people to live by the spirit of the law rather than the letter of it.

The challenge this poses is that it leaves people uncertain what to do. Deciding a 'reasonable rate of interest' is very subjective: it was easier for governments to set a figure. A 1571 English Act of Parliament accepted interest charges of up to 10%. In the following decades, the practice of usury lost much of its moral stigma. Norman Jones comments that, whereas in the medieval world usury was seen as the epitome of greed and oppression, by the seventeenth century 'the matter had become relegated to the status of a theological scruple in a world that accepted lending at interest as an economic necessity'.[33] The post-Reformation world (and that means also the post-Reformation church, including, eventually, the Roman Catholic Church) accepts interest. Or does it? Not entirely.

Islam remains unequivocal on the subject. Interest on loans is forbidden, based on prohibitions in Suras 2, 3, 4 and 30 of the Quran. This does not mean that all Muslims practise interest-free economics. Individual Muslims in the West make accommodation in different ways. Some give anything they receive in interest to charity; others regard themselves as exempt from Quranic provisions because they aren't living in an Islamic country.[34] But the legalization of Islamic banks has opened up new possibilities in the UK since 2004. Muslims (and others) can now take advantage of sharia-compliant financial packages. The theory is that any 'profit' accruing from an account is the result of a risk-taking investment.[35]

Some Christians believe that the Muslim world is putting the West to shame, and that Calvin made a momentous mistake in accepting the charging of interest. Prominent among these are the thinkers associated with the Cambridge-based Jubilee Centre, notably Michael Schluter and Paul Mills.

Jubilee economics: debt versus equity

Paul Mills is an economist who has worked for the International Monetary Fund. In a Cambridge Paper published in March 2011, he explores the self-destructive tendency of a debt-based financial system: a lesson brought home starkly by the global crisis, which revealed the extent to which governments and banks as well as companies and individuals are immersed in debt. He notes that the system has only survived through the debt-based structure and its banks 'holding the economy hostage', passing the costs of their failures on to 'ill-informed or powerless third parties'.[36] These include:

- unpaid creditors in bankruptcies
- taxpayers, through subsidizing company indebtedness, bailing out banks deemed 'too big to fail' or lending to other countries that threaten to default
- savers required to accept low or negative rates of return to bail out borrowers further.

All this, he argues, is 'to stop the house of debt from collapsing'.[37] The system institutionalizes injustice and exploitation.

Mills believes that there is a better way, but 'to follow it requires the courage to question the very foundations upon which finances have been built for the past four centuries. Rather than radical innovation, it means going back to how the church understood finance for the first three-quarters of its history'.[38] He believes that a proper understanding of the biblical texts reveals their relational intent. The prohibitions on interest reinforced the closeness of relationships within the Israelite community. Because Jesus universalized the command to love, and indeed advocated lending without any expectation of return in Luke 6:34–35, Mills and Schluter believe the charging of interest is fundamentally wrong: 'to charge interest to a borrower indicates that the lender does not regard that person as part of their relational community.'[39]

Mills recognizes some would claim that Jesus overturned the Old Testament prohibition of interest. The similar parables of the Talents (Matthew 25:14–30) and the Pounds (Luke 19:11–27) are often cited to support the view that Jesus implicitly sanctioned the taking of interest – because the lazy servant is condemned by his master for not investing his money with the bankers, so that 'on my return I would have received what was my own with interest' (Matthew 25:27). Brian Griffiths, the high-profile Christian banker who is Vice-President of Goldman Sachs International, is one of many who take that view.[40] But Mills takes 'a contrary reading'[41] of the texts. He draws attention to the fact that the servant describes his master as a harsh man who reaps where he does not sow, and the master appears to accept this description (Matthew 25:24–25). By responding that if such is the servant's view, he should have invested the money with the bankers, the master indicates that taking interest from bank deposits is a case of reaping where one hasn't sown.

I take a different view from both Mills and Griffiths. What exactly is the connection between the third servant's unwillingness to trade with his talent and his view of his master as a harsh man who reaps where he does not sow and gathers where he does not scatter? The most plausible explanation is that the servant objects to the fact that any profit or benefit he may derive by trading will be not his, but his master's. The master will reap from the servant's industry and enterprise without doing any work. So the servant is demotivated and hides his talent in the ground. The servant is probably being unfair to the master, but that is the logic of his words and actions. The master then responds by saying: if that's how you view me, then you ought at least to have invested my money with the bankers. The servant is thereby spared from having to do any work (so will *not* do any sowing) but the master still benefits by accruing interest.

It's unfortunate that this parable is viewed as a judgment on the practice of charging interest, both in a positive sense by supporters of capitalism and negatively by capitalism's critics. They misinterpret the parable in opposite ways. Jesus is not making a judgment one way or the other about the morality of interest; the investment with the bankers is simply a detail of the story.

Mills believes that the biblical corollary to the critique of debt-based finance is that 'financial investments that explicitly share profit and loss through partnerships or equity are positively encouraged, as long as any reasonable profit is fairly obtained'.[42] In equity finance, shareholders exercise ownership responsibilities and accept the risk of loss if the business struggles. Mills finds biblical support for this in its lack of presumptuousness. Under God, we should take a humble attitude towards the future for only he knows it with certainty (Proverbs 27:1); boasting about our business plans and the money we are going to make is evil (James 4:13–16). Mills also finds biblical permission for deriving a return from property through rental contracts and leases (Exodus 22:14–15; Leviticus 25:14–16, 29–31).

Private equity investment certainly has the virtue of greater personal involvement. It is no surprise that this appeals to the Jubilee writers with their strong emphasis on relationships.[43] Holders of equity are much more hands-on than shareholders in a public limited company (PLC); they know the people who manage the company and take a more informed concern in how it is run. The relationship between shareholders and managers in PLCs is indirect (often non-existent) by comparison. I shall look at issues of company structure in more detail in chapter 7. Suffice it to say now that if one effect of the financial crisis is to encourage enthusiasm for equity finance and a shift away from reliance on debt-based finance, that is a welcome development.

However, we must retain a sense of proportion. There are disadvantages in equity financing, just as in debt financing. It is true that a bank loan normally requires a business to pay interest from the outset, when start-up costs are considerable. In contrast, equity finance allows entrepreneurs to get under way without a burden of debt. But in due course equity partners will expect a share of the profits, whereas banks only require that their loans be repaid. 'Angel' investors or venture capitalists usually expect a high return on their investment. Their ownership of a substantial share of the company is two-edged: a business may benefit from equity partners' advice, expertise and involvement, but they can also be a source of irritation, hassle and pressure. Much depends on the quality of relationships involved, and on genuinely shared vision and values.

A wise businessperson will weigh the pros and cons of both types of financing carefully in deciding what suits their particular company and personality best. Availability of finance also comes into the equation. I look forward to a day when there is more relational investment in relational companies. In the meantime, however, it is difficult to envisage a situation where there is enough equity capital for every aspiring business.

I would strike a further note of caution in relation to Mills' desire to turn the clock back 500 years. We need to note what has happened during that half millennium. Despite the Western financial system's proneness to crises, bubbles and scandals, it has played a significant part in bringing millions of people out of poverty. Niall Ferguson, who is as critical as anyone of the system's recent failings, counsels a sense of historical perspective:

> Far from being the work of mere leeches intent on sucking the life's blood out of indebted families or gambling with the savings of widows and orphans, financial innovation has been an indispensable factor in man's advance from wretched subsistence to the giddy heights of material prosperity that so many people know today. The evolution of credit and debt was as important as any technological innovation in the rise of civilization, from ancient Babylon to present-day Hong Kong.[44]

Through the process of borrowing and lending, money goes a lot further. Rather than standing idle or inert in a bank vault, it is put out to work. People who would not otherwise be able to do so are able to buy houses or start businesses. Clearly, there are dangers of people overextending themselves (taking on loans they have little chance of repaying) and of unscrupulous financiers exploiting their weakness. We will see further evidence of this in chapter 7. But the charging of interest *can* represent a fair commercial arrangement from which both lender and borrower benefit.

Bribes and gifts

The Old Testament also has much to say about the giving of bribes – a persistent practice in the contemporary world. In his outstanding book on the subject, American scholar John T. Noonan describes a bribe as 'an inducement improperly influencing the performance of a public function meant to be gratuitously exercised'.[45] He demonstrates that down the centuries the core meaning of the word has remained constant, though the specific constituent elements (for example, exactly what is meant by 'inducement' or 'improperly') change from culture to culture. Noonan observes that bribes come both openly and covertly, in all shapes and sizes as sex, commodities, appointments or cash: 'In the shape of sex, bribes have been both male and female, a slave, a wife, a noble boy. As commodities, they have included bedspreads, cups, dogs, fruit, furniture, furs, golf balls, jewels, livestock, peacocks, pork, sturgeon, travel, wine – the gamut of enjoyable goods.'[46]

A bribe these days may consist of securing a relative a position in a prestigious organisation or university in a developed country. The essence of bribery lies not in the specifics of the inducement (that will vary from individual to individual), but in *whether it has the power to distort a person's judgment*.

This is a point that emerges clearly from study of the Old Testament material. The references in the Torah are unequivocal:

- 'You shall take no bribe, for a bribe blinds the officials, and subverts the cause of those who are in the right' (Exodus 23:8).
- 'You shall not render an unjust judgment; you shall not be partial to the poor or defer to the great; with justice you shall judge your neighbour' (Leviticus 19:15).
- 'For the Lord your God is God of gods and Lord of lords, the great God, mighty and awesome, who is not partial and takes no bribe' (Deuteronomy 10:17).
- 'Cursed be anyone who takes a bribe to shed innocent blood' (Deuteronomy 27:25).

The priest Samuel is a man of integrity, who protests his innocence by asking rhetorically 'from whose hand have I taken a bribe to blind my eyes with it? (1 Samuel 12:3). In contrast, his sons 'did not follow in his ways, but turned

aside after gain; they took bribes and perverted justice'
(1 Samuel 8:3).

Condemnation of bribery is a frequent refrain in the
prophets, especially those of the eighth century BC, Isaiah,
Amos and Micah. Bribes are castigated along with the sins of
neglect and decadence in the lives of rulers, judges, priests
and even fellow-prophets:

- 'Your princes are rebels and companions of thieves.
  Everyone loves a bribe and runs after gifts. They do not
  defend the orphan, and the widow's cause does not
  come before them' (Isaiah 1:23).
- 'Aha, you who are heroes in drinking wine and valiant
  at mixing drink, who acquit the guilty for a bribe, and
  deprive the innocent of their rights!' (Isaiah 5:22–23).
- 'For I know how many are your transgressions, and
  how great are your sins – you who afflict the righteous,
  who take a bribe, and push aside the needy in the gate'
  (Amos 5:12).
- 'Its rulers give judgement for a bribe, its priests teach for
  a price, its prophets give oracles for money' (Micah 3:11).
- 'Their hands are skilled to do evil; the official and the
  judge ask for a bribe, and the powerful dictate what
  they desire; thus they pervert justice' (Micah 7:3).

Each strand of biblical material – law, prophecy and historical
narrative – is united in condemning bribery because it results
in a perversion of judgment. The lure of personal gain sways
decisions that should be made on impartial grounds. Bribery
is a violation of high standards of public service. It is a betrayal
of trust.

Most of the references in the Old Testament are judicial.
The prophets were concerned that accepting bribes would

pervert a judge's judgment, so that the guilty (often the rich) were acquitted or the innocent (usually the poor) convicted. The judge's capacity to weigh the evidence objectively would be jeopardized: he should show no partiality. Is this relevant to a business context over 2,500 years later? I believe it is.

In the case of a Government minister or civil servant assessing the merits of rival corporate tenders, there is a similar need for cool impartiality. Such decisions should be decided by criteria relevant to the contract, like quality, cost and timing – in short, value for public money. They should not be decided by how much money is going into private bank accounts, or any other inducement. As anti-corruption campaigner George Moody-Stuart wrote, 'when personal gain becomes a factor, it rapidly becomes the main factor and others pale into insignificance.'[47] The company that *deserves* to supply the goods and services – the one which would serve the needs of the developing countries best – is less likely to win the contract in a bribe-ridden climate.

However, the book of Proverbs seems more ambiguous about bribery. It contains six references, three of them negative and three of them positive:

- 'Those who are greedy for unjust gain make trouble for their households, but those who hate bribes will live' (Proverbs 15:27).
- 'The wicked accepts a concealed bribe in secret to pervert the course of justice' (Proverbs 17:23).
- 'Oppressing the poor in order to enrich oneself, and giving to the rich, will lead only to loss' (Proverbs 22:16).
- 'A bribe is like a magic stone in the eyes of those who give it; wherever they turn they prosper' (Proverbs 17:8).
- 'A gift opens doors; it gives access to the great' (Proverbs 18:16).

- 'A gift in secret averts anger; and a concealed bribe in the bosom, strong wrath' (Proverbs 21:14).

It is largely on the basis of these verses that South African Daryl Balia views the Bible as sending 'mixed messages' on the subject of bribery.[48] How do we make sense of this apparent contradiction? Three comments are in order.

First, the proverbs that strike a positive note about bribes should probably be understood as descriptive, not prescriptive. They describe the reality of life as we know it: in many societies bribery works. Many proverbs make social observation rather taking an explicit moral stance. They offer street-wise wisdom.

Second, inasmuch as moral judgments are being made, underlying issues of power affect how bribery is viewed. The Malaysian Methodist bishop Hwa Yung points out:

> Every condemnation of bribery in the Bible is directed either at those who practise it to pervert justice, or those who use their positions of power to oppress others, especially the poor. We do *not* find a single condemnation of those who have to pay because they are in a position of weakness and are forced to do so.[49]

Bernard Adeney makes a similar point. The equivocation we find in Proverbs:

> seems to reflect a recognition of the power differential between a poor person who gives a gift in order to stave off injustice and the rich who uses his power to exploit the poor. The powerful and the powerless are not judged by the same abstract absolute, but by the relationships and intentions of their situation.[50]

Third, Bible translators are justified in using the word 'bribe' when the sense is negative and 'gift' when it is positive. The word *mattan* employed in Proverbs 18:16 and 21:24 (though not 17:8) is different from *shohad* which is used in the other instances. *Shohad* is more negative in feel. Most cultures distinguish between gifts and bribes. Gifts express friendship and goodwill, intended to further the relationship; are usually made openly and directly; are often reciprocal – gifts are exchanged; and are not intended to create an *obligation* to provide special treatment. In some cultures, such as Japan, the giving and receiving of gifts is of great social significance, and ignoring this jeopardizes the development of relationships.

Nevertheless, care is needed. Gifts may not be understood in the same way on both sides. The more attractive the gift in the mind of the recipient, the likelier it is that it *will* create a sense of obligation. The more I enjoy the beautiful painting, exotic holiday or round of golf accompanied by a superb meal, the greater the possibility that my capacity for coolly assessing the business proposition that follows may be affected.

Grand corruption and petty corruption

A widely accepted definition of corruption is that it is 'the misuse of public power for private gain'.[51] This covers officials in a wide range of positions, high and low, including ministers in national government, civil servants, immigration officials, administrators in local government, directors of public companies, police, judges and magistrates. The payments representing a misuse of their office vary hugely, both in size and significance. So alongside the distinction between bribes and gifts, many make a further distinction between *special* payments and *customary* payments. The latter are also called facilitation payments or, in the USA, 'grease'. Special payments are those that involve paying a bribe to get something immoral, unjust or illegal done. They entail the perversion of judgment that is at the heart of the anti-bribery ethic in the law and the prophets. Examples are the minister of state awarding a big armaments contract on the basis of a payment into his Swiss bank account, or an East African policeman being slipped a wad of notes in order to turn a blind eye to the felling and burning of trees for charcoal, which is then sold by roadsides illegally.

Customary payments are those that expedite the performance of routine business or procedures, and persuade officials to do – more quickly – what they should be doing rather than something they shouldn't. Examples are the small sums paid to customs clerks to get legitimate goods cleared, or to local government officials to persuade them to accept an application registering a new company. Moody-Stuart described the difference as that between 'grand corruption' and 'petty corruption'.[52]

I believe that this is a valid distinction, and in previous discussions about corruption[53] have focused on bribery made at the 'top end' of the scale, by multinational companies seeking to win lucrative contracts. In recent years, many countries have belatedly followed the example of the USA with its 1977 Foreign Corrupt Practices Act, making bribery of foreign officials in order to win or retain business illegal – though doubts persist about their determination in enforcing this. A complicating factor concerns the role played by agents: companies usually secure contracts through middlemen who may pay bribes on their behalf, with or without the companies' full cognizance.

However, my trips to developing countries have made me aware that corruption *within* a country, outside the context of international business, is also a matter of serious moral concern. This sort of corruption affects ordinary citizens most and it is thoroughly irksome.

When I visited Kenya in 2009, I was struck by the extent to which corruption had infiltrated law enforcement agencies. I saw evidence of police corruption first-hand. On the way to Nairobi airport my taxi driver was stopped by a needless police check, and the officer requested a bribe to let us through; the driver refused. It was probably only because he had a white client that the policeman gave way. I was told that routine bribery of police means that they often fail to enforce legislation relating to health, safety and the environment. Thus *matatus*, the mini-buses which are the main form of public transport in Kenya, are seriously overcrowded, and lorries carry heavier loads than they should, damaging the roads.

During my week in Bangalore in 2010, corruption was the staple diet of conversation. I spoke to people from many sectors of business. All agreed that it was a serious problem. This could hardly be denied: a recent survey had declared Bangalore the most corrupt city in India and Karnataka, of which it is capital, the fourth most corrupt state. Here corruption was felt most keenly at the level of local government, especially in submission of applications and renewal of licences. While refusal to pay a bribe did not necessarily mean a registration would be ultimately unsuccessful, it meant a lengthy wait, maybe a year or more. Paying this sort of bribe perverts judgment to some extent, allowing one to jump ahead of others in the paperwork chain.

Indian Christians hold different views about how to respond. At a day seminar on 'God on Monday: Christians Facing Challenges at Work' in which I participated, retired Indian administrator Dr Shantakumari Sunder urged

Christians to take a strong anti-bribery stance; despite difficulties she had faced for going 'against the stream', she had
managed to rise within the Indian Administration Service.
Some delegates agreed. Others felt that some accommodation to the prevailing culture was necessary to maintain
any sort of business presence.[54]

Hwa Yung describes the distinction between grand corruption and petty corruption as one entailing *active* corruption
and the other involving *passive* acceptance within a corrupt
system. While he advocates avoidance of the latter as much
as possible, his view is that total avoidance is impossible in
certain cultures. He also thinks that a careful reading of the
Bible shows that while God's moral demands are absolute, a
certain degree of accommodation to human weakness is
found in the way that they are applied in real-life situations
– from the mixed message of Proverbs on bribery through
to acceptance of polygamy and slavery at certain periods in
history.[55]

Hwa Yung applauds Christians who are able to tell marvel-
lous stories of how they have defied the odds and been able
to avoid paying bribes. But he strikes two notes of caution.
First, these are usually mature Christians and it would be
unreasonable to expect the same of younger believers.
Second, they are often people in upper business echelons with
friends in high places, not humble workers such as taxi drivers
and merchandise sellers.

I respect the opinion of this wise Malaysian bishop. Those
of us in relatively incorrupt countries should be sympathetic
to the plight of people in societies which suffer from endemic
corruption, and be wary of laying upon them burdens heavier
than we ourselves could bear (cf. Matthew 23:4). However, it
is important that in the midst of the darkest situation
Christians seek to be salt and light, mitigating the worst

effects of evil, working for what improvement they can. Even petty bribes should never be paid routinely and willingly; complaints about the officials extorting them should be lodged, as courage and wisdom dictate.

At the seminar in Bangalore, some light shone through the gloom. One was the realization that, rather than viewing local government as a 'no go' area because of its reputation, churches should encourage members with integrity to consider whether God might be calling them to serve there, to help raise standards of behaviour. A second was the observation that an increasing amount of corporate registration and licensing could now be done online; this avoids the need for 'extra' payments, taking out the human, corruptible element. Both offered some hope.

The Corruption Perceptions Index

The anti-corruption organization Transparency International (TI) produces an annual Corruption Perceptions Index. This index ranks perceived levels of corruption among public officials in 177 of the world's 195 countries according to the perceptions of informed observers, mainly businesspeople, political analysts and foreign aid workers. It draws on fifteen different data sources. Though clearly not a definitive, undisputed tool of measurement, the TI Index is widely used and, in Balia's words, 'offers a glimpse of the world map of corruption'.[56]

Countries are rated on a score covering the spectrum from 10 (least corrupt) to 0 (most corrupt). The 2010 list is headed by Denmark, New Zealand and Singapore on 9.3, with Finland and Sweden close behind on 9.2. The bottom four places are filled by Somalia on 1.1, Afghanistan and Myanmar on 1.4, and Iraq on 1.5. Incidentally, India comes 87th, with 3.3. and Kenya 154th with 2.1. What is truly disturbing about the list is the much heavier concentration of countries in the bottom half than the top half. Every country scoring 5 or less has a serious corruption problem, and this is true of no less than 130 countries. Of the ten biggest oil nations in the world (measured by reserve), seven are ranked in the bottom third of the Index – a real challenge for the large petroleum companies.

Some might be sceptical that, once a country has acquired a reputation for corruption (or indeed for being spotlessly clean), it is difficult to dislodge perceptions. The Index could be perpetuating out-of-date impressions. Yet there have been some significant changes over the years. Nigeria, once considered the nadir of corruption, has improved slightly during the last decade. It now ranks 134th equal.[57] Chile has worked its way up to twenty-first and is now considered the least corrupt South American country. On my visit there I was told by two different people: 'Do not try to bribe a Chilean policeman. Not only will he not accept the bribe; he will arrest you for offering it.' This struck me as distinctly encouraging!

Looking further back, a cathartic cultural transformation occurred in Hong Kong during the 1970s and 1980s. The turning-point came with the establishment of an effective Independent Commission Against Corruption by the colonial governor Sir Murray MacLehose in 1973. Its success is attributable to substantial, sustained funding, reflecting the Government's determination to persevere in eliminating corruption.[58] The development of Hong Kong and Singapore as leading financial and commercial centres during the last forty years is surely connected to their being far and away the 'cleanest' cities in Asia. A fatalistic attitude of 'the culture will never change' may be an understandable response, but it is a clear enemy of progress. We can draw hope from countries that prove a national culture *can* change for the better.

A mixed picture

The issues of debt and corruption illustrate the ongoing relevance of the Old Testament to today's global economy. Although contexts have changed, and application of a rigid nature is inappropriate, the underlying principles of biblical law are demonstrably valid.

What, overall, was the outcome of God's concentrating his investment of hope in the people of Israel? The Old Testament presents a mixed picture. There are individuals, groups and episodes where we glimpse life as God intended it: that state of shalom of which the psalmist speaks when:

> [s]teadfast love and faithfulness will meet;
> righteousness and peace will kiss each other.
> Faithfulness will spring up from the ground,
> And righteousness will look down from the sky.
> The Lord will give what is good,
> And your land will yield its increase.
> (Psalm 85:10–12)

On the whole, however, this glorious vision proved tantalizingly elusive. Despite detailed instruction in the law about how to regulate the economy, and regular reminders from the prophets of how the divided nation was falling short, God's chosen people caused him acute frustration. For those of us who are not Jews, this is no reason to feel smugly critical; it is difficult to imagine any other nation doing better. The failings of the Hebrew people were symptomatic of human sinfulness in general. In the prophecy of Jeremiah, the divine discontent reached the point where God again talks in terms of making a fresh start.

> The days are surely coming, says the Lord, when I will make a new covenant with the house of Israel and the house of Judah . . . I will put my heart within them, and I will write it on their hearts; and I will be their God, and they shall be my people.
> (Jeremiah 31:31, 33)

6. HOPE IN A SON: HELPING THE MARGINALIZED

> Long ago God spoke to our ancestors in many and various
> ways, but in these last days he has spoken to us by a Son,
> whom he appointed heir of all things, through whom he
> also created the worlds.
> (Hebrews 1:1–2)

God's appeal to his people through his special messengers, the prophets, had largely fallen on deaf ears. Some, like Jeremiah and Zechariah, met persecution or death.[1] God's enterprise was in a mess. Drastic situations require drastic solutions. Jesus Christ was God's highly original answer.

We have already seen how Proverbs describes wisdom at work in God's great act of creation. In this next episode of the drama, wisdom comes down to earth – literally. Jesus was not simply one more prophet God used to try and drag his chosen people back to their senses. Jesus belonged in the very personhood of God. This was not something his earthly contemporaries realised straightaway. It was a truth that dawned on them gradually, as they came to evaluate Jesus in the light of his whole career. Thus the apostle John came to understand Jesus as the Word, who was with God and actually was God; as the true light that enlightens everyone; and, most remarkably of all, as the *Word made flesh*, full of grace and truth (John 1:1–2, 9, 11). Incarnation describes this act whereby God became man.

To use a metaphor from motor engineering, in Jesus we see God pulling off the wraps and revealing a new prototype.

The first model, Adam, had proved a disappointing failure. A revolution in design was needed. St Paul makes the contrast between the first man, Adam, who was from the dust, and the second man, Christ, who is from heaven (1 Corinthians 15:47; cf. Romans 5:12–19). Jesus had a pre-incarnate existence shared by no-one else. But in his life on earth he entered into our full humanity. Controversy, vulnerability and danger surrounded the start of his life.[2] He, Mary and Joseph experienced the toil, tears and sweat which are the common human lot.

Getting your hands dirty

Joseph was a craftsman. The inhabitants of Nazareth say of Jesus, 'Is not this the carpenter's son?' (Matthew 13:53), though the Greek word *tekton* can be used of a builder in stone as much as a worker in wood. A son usually followed his father's craft, so unsurprisingly the parallel passage in Mark calls Jesus 'the carpenter, the son of Mary . . . ?' (Mark 6:3). The incarnation shows God's readiness to get his hands dirty.

As a carpenter, this must have been literally true. The nineteenth-century pre-Raphaelite artist John Everett Millais painted Christ in the carpenter's shop, with Mary comforting him and removing a splinter from his hand; his cousin John brings him a jug of water to soothe the wound. The picture may strike some as sentimental, and it provoked a vitriolic attack from Charles Dickens, Millais' contemporary,[3] but it illustrates the point that Jesus' working life will have been marked by 'thorns and thistles' just like the rest of us. Not only is he likely to have had its share of physical pain, but challenging relationships as well: one can imagine Jesus having to cope with suppliers providing sub-standard materials, or customers not paying on time. Jesus was about thirty years old when he 'began his work' (Luke 3:23) – by which Luke means began his teaching and healing ministry. But until that time we can assume that Jesus was hard at work in a preparatory sense, learning the ways of human beings through exposure to the nitty-gritty demands of everyday life.

'Getting your hands dirty' is something that people in business know only too well. It means a willingness to be involved in all parts of a job, including those that are unpleasant, backbreaking, difficult and morally complex. Some people turn their noses up at business because of an unwillingness to besmirch themselves. This was especially true of the academic world in the UK a generation ago.

In his autobiography *Beyond Business*, John Browne, Chief Executive of British Petroleum (BP) from 1995 to 2007, includes this fascinating reflection:

> It was a few weeks before I graduated from Cambridge when I was made to understand vividly that business was not held in high regard. June 1969: I had made a comment about considering a career in business, which prompted a reaction from one of my great and distinguished professors, Brian Pippard. While walking along King's Parade with a group of friends, I saw him coming towards us. He turned towards his colleague and said: 'This is Browne. He is going to be a captain of industry. Isn't that amusing?'
>
> His jibe was at both me and business. I was one of the few who had achieved a First in Physics that year. Good students, if they were fascinated by the challenge of science and pursuit of knowledge, were expected to stay on to do a research degree and become academics.
>
> A well-regarded alternative for those not attracted to academic life, or not quite good enough to make the grade, was to take the Civil Service examinations and enter government service. Banking was fine, as long as your family

was actually in banking. Law was perfectly acceptable as was medicine. Compared to these choices, finance – called a 'job in the City' in those days – was regarded as an inferior occupation. But it was still superior to a career in business. There was an unspoken but firm prejudice in the Cambridge environment that business was a waste of potential for high-fliers. It was considered vulgar.[4]

Undeterred by this snobbery, Browne left Cambridge to join BP. He was promptly posted to Anchorage, Alaska, which wasn't quite what he had been expecting.

The Alaskan oil-boom had attracted hordes of single, opportunist, get-rich young men . . . Nightly binge drinking in sawdust-floored bars would often end up in brawls in the street. I certainly began to learn more about life. The streets were piled with snow in the winter and when break-up came, as temperatures soared in the spring, they were a sea of mud.[5]

Nevertheless, Browne rolled up his sleeves and got stuck in, learning his trade on the BP drilling rigs. Like the young boy Jesus in the temple (Luke 2:46), he asked lots of questions and impressed by his eagerness to learn and willingness to break new ground.

Jesus' mission statement: the Nazareth Manifesto
One of my odder habits is that, for a time at least, I collected company mission statements. Eager to discover what companies proclaimed, I accumulated about fifty before my enthusiasm waned. Although many mission statements have a tired and rather derivative feel about them, they sometimes hit on profound truths – when they don't serve simply as a

public relations exercise. For example, I like GlaxoSmithKline's mission statement: 'We have a challenging and inspiring mission to improve the quality of human life by enabling people to do more, feel better and live longer.'[6] It would be difficult to improve on this as a description of what pharmaceutical companies should be about. Enabling people to do more, feel better and live longer: we can all say amen to that. Keep that as your mission and any worker in the drugs industry has a worthwhile vocation. Christian faith should keep people alert to the big picture.

Near the beginning of Luke's Gospel (4:16–20) is what some theologians call the Nazareth Manifesto – Jesus' mission statement.[7] I know many businesspeople who are inspired by it. Jesus has just undergone the pivotal experiences which kick-started his ministry: his baptism by John, temptation in the wilderness and empowerment by the Holy Spirit. On his return to Galilee he takes the opportunity to set the agenda for what will follow, mapping out his programme and indicating his priorities.

The scene is a Saturday morning in the synagogue at Nazareth. Jesus was probably invited to speak because he had started to make a name for himself as an authoritative interpreter of Scripture (Luke 4:15), though not one who was the pupil of any particular Rabbi.

Jesus chooses to read Isaiah 61:1–2:

> The Spirit of the Lord is upon me,
> because he has anointed me
> to proclaim good news to the poor.
> He has sent me to proclaim release to the captives
> and recovery of sight to the blind,
> to let the oppressed go free,
> to proclaim the year of the Lord's favour.

Jesus didn't need to invent a mission statement; he finds one ready-made in the Old Testament. This passage suited his purposes perfectly, to the extent that he says, 'Today this Scripture has been fulfilled in your hearing.' The promise of good times no longer lay in the future; it was being fulfilled in the present – 'today' – and in his person. He is the Lord's Servant of whom the book of Isaiah speaks. He is the one anointed by the Spirit, the longed-for Messiah. So, echoing Isaiah, he promises good things to four groups of people.

Good news to the poor

The poor were those with few possessions and for whom mere survival was a struggle: a day labourer, landless tenant or beggar. But Jesus had a wider understanding which included the poor 'in spirit',[8] those who felt wretched, had low self-esteem and found it difficult to believe that anyone loved them. There was probably a considerable overlap between the materially poor and the spiritually poor. The good news Jesus brought is that God loves those who *are* poor and also those who *feel* poor. This is a love shown both in words, proclaiming the message of salvation, and in deeds, helping the poor become less poor, through a redistribution of wealth. Jesus frequently urged the better-off to give generously to those in need. 'Sell your possessions, and give alms' (Luke 12:33); 'sell all that you own, and distribute the money to the poor' (Luke 18:22). Jesus' focus concurs with the second goal for Christian business stated in the introductory chapter, reducing poverty.

Release to the captives

An alternative translation is 'freedom for the prisoners'. Here it is likely that Jesus was using language metaphorically. So far as we know, people were not released from prison as a result of Jesus' ministry (Barabbas was an unusual exception). Jesus did release men and women from the chains of sin, fear, self-hatred and social marginalization. In addition, there may be a reference to release from debt. Some scholars[9] think that Luke 4:19 alludes to the year of Jubilee, the 'year of God's favour' that occurred once every fifty years. Leviticus 25 describes what this involved: the release of people from various types of debt, the liberation of slaves, rest for the land (being allowed to lie fallow), and the restoration of people to their original family property.[10]

Recovery of sight to the blind

This phrase doesn't actually occur in the original Hebrew of Isaiah 61. Jesus appears to have added it from Isaiah 42:7, the Servant passage which speaks of a 'light to the nations'. There are several instances in the Gospels of Jesus enabling blind people to see (for example, Mark 8:22–26; Mark 10:46–52; John 9:1–12). The restoration of any of the senses is clearly life-transforming. Moreover, Jesus used sight as a metaphor for spiritual perception: understanding the truth about himself, God and the human condition (for example, Luke 6:39, 10:23–24). People who can see physically may be blind at a deeper level. So he calls his religious opponents, the scribes and the Pharisees, 'blind guides', because they 'strain out a gnat but swallow a camel'; they are obsessed with the minutiae of the law (tithing mint, dill and cumin) while neglecting the 'weightier matters of the law' – justice and mercy and faith (Matthew 23:23–24).

Freedom for the oppressed

The 'oppressed' are those who are pressed down and therefore heavily laden. This takes many forms: economic oppression (employers paying workers little or nothing), mental oppression (evil spirits possessing vulnerable people) or religious oppression (teachers imposing on the public a fastidious understanding of the law). Jesus brought freedom at all these different levels. He promised his disciples: 'Come to me, all you that are weary and are carrying heavy burdens, and I will give you rest' (Matthew 11:28). Those whose lives he transformed included Mary Magdalene, rid of the seven demons that had tormented her (Luke 8:2); Zacchaeus, inspired to refund those he had defrauded, which would help them financially (Luke 19:8); and all who heeded his message that the law was given for human welfare, not to trap and imprison them (Mark 2:23–28).[11]

Taken together, these four aspects of Jesus' ministry amount to a demonstration of *the Lord's favour*. If the poor, the captives, the blind and the oppressed are receiving such blessing, they are receiving a fresh taste of God's goodness. Jesus was saying: this is a bumper year – wake up to it!

This is a compelling passage of Scripture. The Christian consultancy Tricordant[12] see their calling to bring wholeness to dysfunctional and demoralized organizations in the light of Luke 4:18–19. It inspired solicitor James Featherby during the many years he worked for the City legal firm Slaughter & May. In a conference at Ridley, he admitted it might be thought unlikely that one would find the poor, prisoners and oppressed working in the City, but he knew many examples of desperately needy individuals:

- those struggling with inadequate resources
- people suffering from a mid-life crisis
- the objects of bullying, gossip and manipulation
- those who have lost touch with their feelings and can't apologize

- grumblers, people who over-drink, have no time for their families and can't turn off their mobiles, or are driven by targets or their own egos.[13]

But the businesspeople most closely following the Nazareth Manifesto are those whose employees and customers resemble the socially marginalized people that Jesus had in view. They are the social entrepreneurs, people who run companies that have the transformation of society, the reduction of poverty or environmental sustainability as explicit goals.

One example is the group of Christians who run SonLight Power, an American company that promotes solar-powered energy in developing countries, notably Honduras. Kevin Sasson, who left a successful career in Silicon Valley to become executive director, says that SonLight's power systems are often installed at off-grid primary schools, which 'provide venues for community events, adult education classes, medical clinics, and communication hubs'.[14] SonLight trains local residents in the basics of renewable energy and how to maintain their new solar electric system, thus ensuring sustainability. The name of the company is a testimony to its inspiration – the Son of God who is the Light of the World.

Jesus' strapline: the kingdom of God

A single phrase dominates the teaching of Jesus as recorded in the synoptic Gospels of Matthew, Mark and Luke.[15] It is *the kingdom of God*. If Luke 4:18–19 is Jesus' mission statement, then the kingdom of God is the nearest Jesus comes to a company strapline.

Intriguingly, for all Jesus' talk about the kingdom, he never defines it. Jesus says what it is *like* rather than what it *is*. His favourite device when preaching about the kingdom is to tell a parable; Matthew 13 contains no less than seven parables which begin 'the kingdom is like . . . ' In addition, the kingdom is illustrated by Jesus' deeds as well as his words; he embodied the kingdom in what he did, the attitudes he displayed, and the impact he had on people's lives.[16]

The parables of the kingdom abound with illustrations taken from everyday work. Indeed, the central character is usually someone we identify by their occupation. This is just a selection from Jesus' impressive cast:

- a farmer going out to sow (Mark 4:3–9)
- a woman making bread by mixing yeast with flour (Matthew 13:33)
- a merchant selling possessions to buy a precious stone (Matthew 13:45–46)
- a tower-builder working out his estimates (Luke 14:28–30)
- a shepherd searching for a lost sheep (Luke 15:1–7)
- a middle manager faced with the sack making provision for his future (Luke 16:1–8)
- a harsh judge confronted by a widow pleading for justice (Luke 18:1–8)
- a tax collector being treated with contempt by a Pharisee (Luke 18:9–14)
- a king settling accounts with his slaves (Matthew 18:23–35)
- a vineyard owner coping with unruly tenants (Mark 12:1–9).

Some of these stories feature workers doing exactly what one would expect them to do. Others entail workers doing surprising things that would raise eyebrows and get listeners thinking. Often there is a twist to the tale.

What is Jesus doing with this wealth of workplace imagery? What was his intention, for instance, in telling the parable of the labourers in the vineyard (Matthew 20:1–16)? This is the curious story of the man who employs casual labourers at various different hours of the day (some for the whole day, others for as little as one hour) and who pays all of them the same wage: one denarius. I have heard attempts to draw sharply contrasting lessons for industrial practice from this parable. There is the chief executive's perspective, that employers have absolute authority in this area, and therefore the right to pay employees exactly what they like. Then there is the socialist shop steward's perspective, that all employees should be paid the same, whatever work they do or however hard they work. Finally there is the lawyer's perspective, that so long as an employer sticks by an agreement with an employee, no-one has the right to complain. The Latin Church Fathers Jerome and Augustine took this view. They both reject the claim that the wage settlement was unjust because the vineyard owner paid the agreed sum; the labourers had entered freely into negotiation with him and the owner stayed true to his word. This led both theologians to advocate free bargaining as a means to discerning a just wage.[17]

In reality, it is highly unlikely that Jesus was commending the outcome he describes as sensible commercial practice. Rather, he is deliberately picturing *unusual* practice to highlight God's grace in forgiving and accepting those who repent late in life. In other words, grace is a great equalizer; when it comes to salvation, we all depend on God's favour. Because we human beings are set in a differentials mentality, God's generosity towards those who turn to him at an advanced stage is apt to seem unfair to those who have served him throughout their lives. But this merely underlines the fact that God's mercy transcends all human notions of fairness. Similar comments might be made about many other parables. Jesus is principally concerned with such themes as the relationship between God and human beings, or the importance and urgency of accepting God's offer of salvation.

Nevertheless, I would be loath to suggest that we abandon all attempts to extract some guidance about our working practices from this rich vein of imaginative storytelling. In a Grove Booklet I co-authored with David Clough on *The Ethics of Executive Pay*, we considered the possible relevance of the various parables that Jesus taught about human agents (managers, stewards, tenants or servants) for the vexed issue of corporate governance. While we were wary of reading more into the stories than Jesus intended, we did find certain details highly suggestive, notably:

- the servants are judged on their performance over a lengthy period of time – it is no superficial, short-term assessment (Luke 12:45; Matthew 25:19)
- the judgment that follows is decisive: promotion in some cases, dismissal in others. Sustained long-term performance is rewarded, but there is no toleration of ongoing failure (Luke 12:43–44, 47–48; Matthew 25:16–17, 28)
- the judgment covers both financial performance (in the Matthew 25 parable) and interpersonal behaviour (in the Luke 12 parable).

Long-term, performance-related, decisive and relational: these are all criteria, we proposed, that have their place in the setting of executives' pay packages.[18]

In addition, it is important to note that Jesus took for granted a world of work and exchange where buying and selling are everyday human activities. A recent article on theology and work suggested that Christ's teaching 'appears to have a pronounced hostility towards trading and the accruing of riches'.[19] While Jesus certainly warned against the idolization of money, I see no evidence that he regarded trading *per se* as problematic. Jesus' vividly illustrative style of teaching affirmed the world of work, while simultaneously widening people's horizons and drawing them into a vision of something bigger.

As we assemble the different strands of Jesus' teaching about the kingdom of God, it becomes clear that God's kingdom is where God *reigns* or *rules*. Moreover, it denotes territory where God's rule is acknowledged, where people accept his rule over the whole of their lives. In Jesus' parables, business is more than a much-used metaphor for the kingdom of God. It is a key area of life where God is working to extend his kingdom.

Friend of tax collectors

Jesus' choice of company was unconventional and he found himself in trouble because of it. The scribes and Pharisees noticed Jesus' odd social habits early in his ministry and complained to his disciples, asking 'Why does he eat with tax collectors and sinners?' (Mark 2:16). The issue recurs: 'Now all the tax collectors and sinners were coming near to listen to him. And the Pharisees and the scribes were grumbling and saying, "This fellow welcomes sinners and eats with them"' (Luke 15:1–2). The accusation clearly rankled with Jesus, since he observes of the people of his generation: 'the Son of Man has come eating and drinking, and you say, "Look, a glutton and a drunkard, a friend of tax-collectors and sinners!"' (Luke 7:34). Commentator George Caird comments of the scribes' and Pharisees' attitude: 'His critics believed that their whole duty is to avoid anything that could contaminate their sanctity, and they are bewildered at his disregard of their spiritual security policy.'[20]

Tax collectors worked both for the Romans, who got other people to do their dirty work, and for Herod, who needed money for his ambitious building projects. They were deeply unpopular and barred from synagogues. Jews collected taxes from their fellow-Jews, so they were seen as collaborators and traitors. Three grades of collectors made up a large pyramid system: supervisors at the top, chief tax collectors with responsibility for a particular town or area (like Zacchaeus for Jericho, Luke 19:2) and managers of tollbooths (like Levi by Lake Galilee, Mark 2:14).[21] The collectors paid themselves from the money they collected; the Romans didn't mind collectors charging as much as they liked so long as they passed on an agreed sum.

So this was a group of people who had made themselves rich at the cost of deep unpopularity. In making the effort to socialize with them, Jesus shows that he was not exclusively concerned with the poor. His heart went out to all who were socially marginalized, those who were ostracized and suffered from prejudice. Such prejudice is often illogical or unfair: inasmuch as tax collection serves the common good by raising money for public services, it is a legitimate profession. Someone has to do the 'dirty work', however unpopular; consider the situation of the Jewish money-lenders in medieval Europe.[22] But prejudice that is unfair often gets mixed up with criticism that is justified.

Jesus saw the individual who lay behind the extortionate practice and the social isolation. So he takes the initiative in calling Levi to be a disciple, just as he defies the crowd in addressing Zacchaeus up the sycamore tree and inviting himself to lunch. The fact that he spent time eating and drinking with tax collectors shows Jesus enjoyed their company. Maybe he found their no-nonsense approach and readiness to open up their homes refreshing. Yet Jesus had no illusions about the sickness of the tax collectors' way of life and their need to change. So he defends his practice against his critics by saying, 'Those who are well have no need of a physician, but those who are sick; I have come to call not the righteous but sinners' (Mark 2:17). In Luke 15:11–32 his response to criticism is to tell three parables illustrating God's love for the 'lost': the lost sheep, the lost coin and the lost son.

What is the relevance of this dimension of Jesus' ministry today? Few people are enthusiastic about paying tax, and in some countries there is a deep-seated disillusionment about the prospect of governments putting it to good use. I found this within the Christian community in south India. But in most societies the occupation of tax collector no longer attracts the same opprobrium that it did in Jesus' day. In the UK and USA it is bankers who have now assumed the mantle of tax collectors in terms of incurring unpopularity and public disdain. It was not ever thus. Bankers used to be respected as models of rectitude. That image has changed dramatically as a result of the trends of the last twenty-five years, culminating in the errors of judgment that led to the financial crisis of 2007–9.[23] Bankers have been castigated for pursuing risky policies and arcane practices which, when exposed as unsound, led to a loss of confidence in the system. The fact that government action to shore up several leading banks increased the level of public borrowing to an unsustainable level, and drastic cuts in public spending ensued, has contributed to that unpopularity. Above all, the huge rewards available to people who work in banking leave the general public feeling amazed, aghast and angry.

The Economist summed up the mood well in a article published in May 2011:

In the face of widespread public contempt, banks continue to dole out huge amounts of money to their high fliers. Indeed, Wall Street pays more to its bankers today than it did before the financial crisis. In Europe the banking sector's total wage bill jumped by about 8% last year, overtaking the previous record set in 2007. British investment bankers are doing best of all, with pay in some banks increasing by as much as 20%. It is not only the public who fume at this. Politicians despair that banks can take public bail-outs with one hand and dole out lavish pay with the other.[24]

So bankers are looking like the new social outcasts. In this curious turn of events, Christians must beware of simply following the crowd, joining in the mud-slinging. There are wild accusations that need challenging. When Western governments pumped money into the banks to ensure their survival, it was not primarily to rescue bankers. That action guaranteed the security of deposits made by ordinary members of the public. Not all banks behaved irresponsibly in the lead-up to the crisis; even those with sound financial practices were affected by the deadlock in inter-bank lending which threatened to bring the system to its knees. The financiers who triggered the crisis were not solely responsible for the escalation of public debt; many governments already had huge deficit budgets. In evaluating responsibility and blame, it is important to make measured judgments and avoid the temptation to scapegoat a particular group. If Jesus went out of his way to show he accepted Zacchaeus, Christians might well emulate him today by befriending a beleaguered banker.

However, Jesus' friendship provoked a revolution in Zacchaeus' attitude. This seems to have happened without Jesus having to lecture him on his moral shortcomings; being in the master's presence over a meal was enough. Zacchaeus is moved to assert: 'Look, half of my possessions, Lord, I will give to the poor; and if I have defrauded anyone of anything, I will pay back four times as much' (Luke 19:8). One would like to hope that this combination of generosity and restitution might inspire those in the banking community. No doubt many are generous in giving some of their wealth to worthy causes.[25] Restitution, in contrast, might strike most bankers as both uncalled for and difficult. Yet inasmuch as their mistakes *did* cause demonstrable suffering to others, they owe the public something. The least they can surely do is show restraint concerning the financial rewards that they expect to muster from their work. In particular, I suggest that bankers do some serious heart-searching about the expectation that they receive both a high basic salary and substantial bonuses. One or the other, maybe; but how do you justify both?[26]

Friend of prostitutes

The labelling of Jesus as a friend of tax collectors and sinners prompts the question as to what sort of people are meant by 'sinners'. The answer is people who persistently and deliberately transgressed the law. Among this group, prostitutes – those who sold themselves to a life of sexual sin – were prominent. Deuteronomy 23:17–18 forbids both female and male temple prostitution, which was associated with pagan fertility cults, while Leviticus 19:29 commands parents: 'Do not profane your daughter by making her a prostitute.' The book of Proverbs warns against wayward women (5:3–5), describing a prostitute as 'a deep pit' (23:27).

In Matthew 21:28–32, Jesus explicitly brackets tax collectors and prostitutes together. He tells a parable of two sons, one who told his father he would work in the vineyard today but failed to do so, and the other who said he wouldn't but did so. Jesus shocks his audience of religious leaders (the chief priests and the elders – see Matthew 21:23) by saying, 'Truly, I tell you, the tax collectors and the prostitutes are going into the kingdom ahead of you. For John came to you in the way of righteousness and you did not believe him, but the tax collectors and the prostitutes believed him.'

We do not know a great deal about prostitution in first-century Palestine, but it probably included independent sex workers and those employed by others, as in most societies throughout history. No doubt hypocrisy surrounded it, outwardly respectable men vilifying women who were prostitutes while making use of their services. Jesus had a keen eye for hypocrisy,[27] and his sympathetic attitude to prostitutes may have stemmed partly from his awareness of the double standards that contribute to their plight.

For detailed information about Jesus' interaction with prostitutes, we are largely dependent on the story of his encounter with the sinful woman who anointed him in Luke 7:36–50. Unfortunately, a certain amount of confusion surrounds this woman's identity. Ever since a speech by Pope Gregory the Great in 591, there has been a tendency to associate her with Mary Magdalene, one of Jesus' closest companions. While this makes for a good storyline and has given rise to much memorable Christian art, portraying Mary with long red hair hanging loose over her voluptuous body,[28] the biblical grounds for it are thin. The story of the sinful woman in Luke 7 is followed closely by the Gospels' first mention of Mary Magdalene as the woman 'from whom seven demons had gone out' in Luke 8:3. If the two women were one and the same, Luke would surely have made that clear.

The incident Luke describes takes place in the house of a Pharisee called Simon. In his commentary, Caird sets the scene superbly:

Simon respected Jesus enough to call him Rabbi and half thought he might be a prophet; he was sufficiently interested in him to invite him to dinner, but received him with formal politeness, without any of the little gestures – the footbath, the kiss, the perfume – which would have betokened a warm welcome. At an oriental banquet the guests left their sandals at the door and reclined on low couches with their feet behind them. It was not uncommon for the doors to be left open to admit all sorts of people, from beggars in search of food to a rabbi's admirers in search of intellectual entertainment.[29]

This is the cue for 'a woman in the city' (prostitution is a mainly urban phenomenon), 'who was a sinner' (enough said), to enter. She had learned that Jesus was eating in the Pharisee's house. We do not know whether she had met Jesus previously. She may have, or perhaps what she had seen and heard of him was enough to explain her actions. She stood behind Jesus with an alabaster jar of ointment, but before she even opens it she starts weeping and then, 'forgetting that this was something a decent woman never did in public',[30] lets down her hair to dry Jesus' feet with her hair. She then kissed and anointed them. Not surprisingly, Simon the Pharisee is appalled, as much by Jesus allowing this as by the woman's actions: 'If this man were a prophet, he would have known who and what kind of woman this is who is touching him – that she is a sinner' (Luke 7:39).

Jesus understands the woman's bathing and drying of his feet as a demonstration of great love, an indication that she has experienced forgiveness. From her knowledge of Jesus the woman had realized that even she, a notorious sinner, can be forgiven, and Jesus goes on to reassure her: 'Your sins are forgiven' (Luke 7:48). Where Simon saw only a sinner, Jesus saw someone who had been pardoned and restored. Through a short parable, Jesus forced from the Pharisee the reluctant admission that the extent of affection shown by a debtor is often related to the size of the debt cancelled (7:40–46).

We do not know what became of this woman afterwards. It would not have been easy for her to change her profession, as few self-respecting men wish to marry a former prostitute, and other work would be hard for a single woman to find. However, it is difficult to imagine her going back to her old ways and continuing as a prostitute after such a profound experience of forgiveness and love. Seeing oneself in a whole new light is often the prelude to a radical change of career.

Prostitution is a significant part of the global economy. It has been calculated that at any given moment, 40 million prostitutes are at work. The industry is especially rampant in Thailand (where it is worth $35 billion) and Japan ($27 billion); this makes the Netherlands, famous for Amsterdam's red-light district, look modest (a mere $1 billion). Prostitution is legal and regulated in twenty-two countries. About 2.5 million people are victims of sex trafficking, with no less than two-thirds of these coming from Eastern Europe.[31]

The scale of the phenomenon is massive, but the good news is that one of the fastest-growing areas of social enterprise in today's world is the provision of alternative employment for sex workers. Christian faith, modelled on the ministry and example of Jesus, provides the inspiration for many of the organizations that are seeking to rescue women from prostitution.

Oasis is a UK-based worldwide organization which seeks to serve and transform communities by promoting inclusion and confronting injustice. It works among poor and marginalized groups in ten countries; its ministry to prostitutes is concentrated in India. In the cities of Mumbai and Bangalore, Oasis staff get to know and befriend street workers, building relationships through a drop-in centre and a halfway home for those wanting to leave prostitution. They alert the police to girls aged under eighteen working in brothels. The police aren't always responsive, but when I visited Bangalore, Oasis staff were jubilant about a successful combined operation in which forty-four girls had been rescued. Oasis next offers the girls and women transitional care and counselling. International Director Andy Matheson describes what happened to Zarine, a girl from Kolkata who was tricked into the sex trade when twelve, worked in a brothel in Mumbai for six years, became HIV-positive and then took the brave decision to leave.

> When she first came out we arranged for her to stay with a family who we thought would create the kind of welcoming atmosphere that she needed, but they couldn't cope with her HIV-positive status and so, once more, she was rejected. Then she went to our newly established community for women and children who had been ostracized because of their HIV status. There, through the love, counsel and training she received, she began to put the pieces of her life back together. A lot happened over the following seven years, but eventually she decided that she wanted to give her life to helping others who had been trafficked into prostitution. And so for the past seven years she has served on our staff doing exactly that.[32]

Another former prostitute, Sarika, took many years to recover from exploitation as a teenager. However, at Purnata Bhavan, an Oasis care home outside Mumbai, she has experienced significant healing. She has learned the skill of Aari (Indian bead-making) work and hopes to practise this in the future.

Alongside the restorative work with prostitutes, Oasis runs enterprises that provide alternative employment for vulnerable young women. I visited Jacobs Well, named after the location where Jesus had a life-changing encounter with a social outcast, the much-married Samaritan woman (John 4:1–30). It is an Oasis India fair trade business initiative in Bangalore which makes a variety of products including clothes, bags and jewellery. Oasis India offers a one-year course for young women, mainly Tamil-speaking Hindus from the slum areas, who show an aptitude for sewing; they are then taught the skills of tailoring, embroidery and pattern cutting, as well as being given an introduction to the Bible and Christianity. Jacobs Well employs course graduates who continue training for a year before they become fully fledged tailors. They also become proficient in team-working, using computers for production planning and communication, and packaging for export. A Wednesday morning Bible study provides a more in-depth look at the Christian faith, conducted sensitively and without pressure; I visited on a Wednesday so was promptly asked to lead! The company offers a genuine alternative for young women from poor backgrounds who might otherwise be sucked into the sex industry.

I went on to visit a community of about seventy women and children run by the Mahalir Aran Trust at Dharmapuri in the neighbouring state of Tamil Nadu. It is led by a truly inspirational Sri Lankan woman, Mercy Imondi, who is supported by her Italian husband Vinci. Mercy visited the area when twenty-one and was so shocked by the 'sexploitation' happening even in a very rural context (she met a prostitute aged nine) that she founded a refuge community for women and girls. Mahalir Aran means 'a place of protection for women'. Most of these women now work for a company, Flowering Desert, which makes beautiful silk shawls, cushion covers, jute bags and greeting cards; I saw them at work on their sewing machines. Mercy is greatly helped in the process of design, product development and production processes by an English art designer, Janet Rogers, who runs a consultancy called VIA Design – VIA standing for Vision, Inspiration and Action. The latest initiative at Dharmapuri is a new on-site medical clinic. I have rarely visited a place which radiated such courage, hard work, joy and hope for the future.

I also came across Christian organizations helping women in the sex industry during my time in Nairobi. Notable among these is Bega kwa Bega, which means 'shoulder to shoulder' in Swahili. Supported by St John's Roman Catholic Church, Bega kwa Bega operates in the extraordinarily over-crowded slum of Korogocho (aptly named, because it means 'confusion'), where 120,000 people are crowded into a single square kilometre without access to piped water or proper sanitation. Its chief mission is to rescue women from working as prostitutes in central Nairobi. If left to continue, many die by thirty from AIDS, botched abortions and alcoholism. It provides alternative employment through the making of sisal baskets, patchwork bags, beads and dolls. The local priest visits every Monday to pray with the women. Directed by Ignatius Mayero, Bega kwa Bega operates essentially as a cooperative self-help society.[33] Like many other worthwhile African enterprises, it has benefited from a loan made by Shared Interest, the social investment company based in Newcastle. This enabled Bega kwa Bega to buy eighteen new sewing machines, bring in more women and buy a laptop and digital camera for Ignatius to help his marketing.

While these various social enterprises are a small drop in a vast ocean, they constitute a genuine sign of hope. They are fully consistent with the mission of the Son of God who spent his time in the most disreputable sections of society. Many people working in the sex industry do so through no desire of their own. They are prostitutes because their families have sold them into that condition, they see no other way to make ends meet or they are in the vice-like grip of criminal gangs. They need our compassion, not our condemnation. Prostitution is a corruption of sex because it makes an act that should be a free gift of love into a commercial transaction. It is therefore both appropriate and encouraging that the best prospect for fighting prostitution is to offer commercial opportunities of other types. Christians doing this are a genuine power for good. They may be getting their hands dirty in a metaphorical sense, but transforming the career prospects of those operating on the moral margins of society is work dear to the heart of Jesus.

The hoped-for Messiah

As Jesus continued his teaching and healing ministry around Galilee, he gathered a loyal band of followers. Among his inner circle of twelve disciples a sense of excitement grew about Jesus' identity. Near the village of Caesarea Philippi Jesus pressed them as to who they thought he was. Simon, who was about to acquire the name Peter, did not hesitate: 'You are the Messiah, the Son of the living God!' (Matthew 16:16).

Jesus accepts this acclamation of his Messianic identity: 'Blessed are you, Simon son of Jonah! For flesh and blood has not revealed this to you, but my Father in heaven' (Matthew 16:17). The Messiah whom the Jews hoped for was a military liberator anointed by God: one who would overthrow the nation's oppressive overlords, restore the Davidic dynasty and inaugurate a kingdom of justice and peace. When Peter saluted Jesus as the Messiah, this was probably the type of leader he hoped Jesus would turn out to be. After Jesus' death, the two disciples on the Emmaus road make a very telling admission: 'we had hoped that he was the one to redeem Israel' (Luke 24:21). Some of Jesus' actions were so astounding, and so reminiscent of the Old Testament liberator Moses, that they excited the crowds to fever pitch – as when they wanted to make him king after the feeding of the 5000 (John 6:14–15).

Yet Jesus' understanding of his identity was very different to popular expectation. Although his disciples included at least one from the revolutionary Zealot faction, Jesus avoided violence. A man who taught his followers to 'turn the other cheek' and 'go the extra mile' (Matthew 5:39–41) was unlikely to lead an insurrection against the Romans. This may be why Judas ultimately betrayed him; he became disillusioned with Jesus.

No sooner was the truth of his Messiahship revealed than Jesus insists his disciples keep it a secret (Matthew 16:20). In addition, he knew that a violent end lay ahead, and rebuked Peter sharply when the latter tried to persuade him otherwise. So clearly does Jesus see the traditional Messiah role as a demonic temptation that his leading disciple experiences in quick succession the joy of being called blessed and the horror of being called Satan (16:23).

In Luke's Gospel a momentous sense of impending destiny pervades the narrative from the time when Jesus resolutely 'set his face to go to Jerusalem' (Luke 9:51). Jesus' most powerful enemies were largely concentrated there. Falling foul of the local scribes and Pharisees in Galilee was one thing; alienating the high priestly family of Annas and Caiaphas, who colluded with the Roman occupiers, was much more dangerous. Jesus was never a man to shirk controversy, and engaging in public debate in the temple could spell serious trouble. As Jesus' disciples realized that he was determined to meet his destiny in the capital, their hopes turned to apprehension: a mood summed up by Thomas, who said fatalistically 'Let us also go, that we may die with him' (John 11:16). Hope in God's Son lay in the balance.

7. THE DEATH AND RESURRECTION OF HOPE: INTEGRITY, SACRIFICE AND VINDICATION

Thomas' forebodings were justified. Jesus' final visit to Jerusalem culminated in his death on a cross.

The question 'why did Jesus die?' can be answered on more than one level, human and divine. The human explanation is that certain individuals and groups in Jerusalem in AD 30 wanted to get rid of Jesus. Matthew clearly identifies the first group: 'Then the chief priests and the elders of the people assembled in the palace of the high priest, who was called Caiaphas, and they conspired to arrest Jesus by stealth and kill him' (Matthew 26:3). Two main motives explain their hatred of Jesus.

The first was *legalism*. Jesus infuriated the religious establishment of his day because they saw him as a lawbreaker. His free interpretation of the sabbath law, his insistence on socializing with notorious sinners, and the claims that he made directly and indirectly about himself all contributed to his image as a lawbreaker to those bent on finding fault – even though he actually fulfilled the law at its deepest level. The religious leaders could not appreciate the new work that God was doing in Jesus. They didn't want to hear the message that God loves and welcomes every sinner who repents. They were legalists.

The second was *jealousy* – a vicious, malevolent spirit of envy. Pilate saw that: 'For he realised that it was out of jealousy that the chief priests had handed him over' (Mark 15:10). They were furious with Jesus, not just because they disagreed with his understanding of the law, but because he was popular. The crowds listened to him and hung on his every word; they went to him with their problems and ailments; and they gave him a royal reception on his arrival in Jerusalem. Jesus had displaced the religious leaders in popular esteem. We should not underestimate the part that bitter personal jealousy played in the events that led to Jesus' crucifixion.

However, the only people with the authority to crucify were the occupying Romans. It was Pontius Pilate who issued the fatal instruction for Jesus to be crucified. He eventually bowed to the pressure of the chief priests and the baying of the fickle crowd: 'When Pilate saw that he could do nothing, but rather that a riot was beginning, he took some water and washed his hands in front of the crowd . . . ' (Matthew 27:24).

His motive was *expediency*. Pilate wanted as quiet a life as governor as possible. A riot would weaken Roman rule. News of it would reach Rome, damaging his reputation and career prospects. So although Jesus appeared a harmless man ('I find no case against him' (John 19:6)), Pilate's self-interest dictated that Jesus be sacrificed.

In addition, the tetrarch Herod Antipas played a significant supporting role. He ruled Galilee as a client state of the Roman Empire. In Acts 4:27 the death of Jesus is attributed to 'Herod and Pontius Pilate, with the Gentiles and the peoples of Israel'. Herod executed John the Baptist, and Jesus, aware of his cunning menace, called him a fox (Luke 13:32). When Pilate learnt that Jesus was a Galilean he sent Jesus to Herod, who was visiting Jerusalem at the time. Herod, ever the playboy, was delighted because he wanted to see Jesus in the hope that he would 'perform some sign' (Luke 23:8). When Jesus refused to comply, Herod and his soldiers treated him with contempt, mocked him and sent him back to Pilate.

Jesus was a victim of the power politics of his day, like many before and since. He was the victim of people and systems conniving against him: Pilate and the Roman empire; Caiaphas and Jewish priestly authority; Herod and the tetrarchal system. Their joint interests dictated that a man who commanded such a strong popular following should be eliminated. Jesus was a good man who did not deserve to die. But he was born into a highly explosive situation. The forces of his time conspired against him.

However, Jesus did not regard death as inevitable because he was on a collision course with religious and political authority. He saw his death as an essential component of his life's work. He spoke of glorifying God on earth by completing the work God had given him (John 17:3).[1] Geoff Shattock, founder of Worktalk, writes: 'We don't tend to think of death as work . . . but for Jesus of Nazareth this six hour period was literally a work "shift" which represented the climax of the work he was born to do.'[2] We will examine why this is so later. For now, let us simply note the fact that Jesus died in the course of his work. Christians believe that his death was a unique event with special saving significance; and the method of his death – by crucifixion – was both extreme and, thankfully, confined to the past. But this does not mean Jesus' death is of no relevance to momentous events that happen in the business world. This is what we will now explore.

Death at work

A spectacular example of businesspeople suffering violent death as a result of evil conspiracy is 9/11.

On 11 September 2001, two planes hijacked by al-Qaeda terrorists ploughed into the twin towers of the World Trade Center. 2,606 people working in the World Trade Center were killed.[3] American Airlines flight 11 hit the North Tower at

8.46 am. Its centre of impact was floors 93–100, which were occupied by Marsh & McLennan Companies, the global professional services and insurance brokerage firm. They lost all 295 employees and sixty contractors who were working there. The firm that took the largest loss of life, however, was financial services company Cantor Fitzgerald, whose corporate headquarters was on floors 101–105. All 658 employees present that morning (about two-thirds of their total workforce) died. At the very top of the building, 164 people who were staff, guests or contractors in the Windows on the World restaurants were killed.

The carnage in the South Tower was not quite so extensive, because many firms started to evacuate the building between 8.46 and 9.03, when the second plane, United Airlines flight 175, struck. However, there was still a major loss of life. The worst-affected company was Aon Corporation, provider of risk management services, insurance and reinsurance, which occupied offices on floors 92 and 98–105, several storeys above the area of impact. Of Aon's employees, 924 evacuated successfully but 175 died.

Some commentators suggested that the attacks revealed the depth of Muslim opposition to global capitalism and US military hegemony, with the World Trade Center and the Pentagon (which was also attacked) being powerful visual symbols of each. For instance, academic Douglas Kellner wrote:

> The targets were partly symbolic, representing global capital and American military power, and partly material, intending to disrupt the airline industry, the businesses centered in downtown New York, and perhaps the global industry itself through potentially dramatic downturns of the world's largest stock market and primary financial center.[4]

However, the primary motives are more likely to have concerned events in the Middle East. Al-Qaeda and their ringleader Osama bin Laden stated US support for Israel, US presence in Saudi Arabia and sanctions against Iraq as reasons for the attacks.[5] It is clear that the hijackers wanted to kill as many Americans as possible; they weren't concerned about which Americans, or indeed that those of other nationalities got caught up in the attack.[6] Whatever the rights or wrongs of US policy in the Middle East, people who worked for commercial organizations in the Twin Towers were not responsible for devising or implementing it. They were innocent victims of an international conspiracy who happened to be working in the wrong place at the wrong time. All the hopes they had invested in their corporate careers were extinguished in an instant. Many had their lives cut short in their prime – just as Jesus did.

More often, people die at work through industrial accidents. The Industrial Labour Organization calculates that, globally, 337 million accidents happen each year, claiming 600,000 lives.[7] In the UK, 152 people died in industrial accidents in 2009–10.[8] Certain industrial disasters are indelibly lodged in the memory because of their huge scale and lasting effects. In 1984, nearly 4,000 people died in the Indian city of Bhopal when a valve in an underground storage tank at the Union Carbide plant broke, releasing methyl isocyanate gas into the atmosphere. An estimated 40,000 individuals were disabled, maimed or suffered serious illness. The worst US industrial accident occurred in 1947 at Texas City, when a fire on board the SS Grandcamp during the loading of 2,300 tons of ammonium nitrate led to a massive explosion; the subsequent chain reaction killed 581 people, injured over 5,000 and destroyed the entire port.

In 2005, Texas City was again in the news for unwelcome reasons when an explosion took place at the BP refinery, killing fifteen and injuring 170. The overfilling of a splitter tower with gasoline led, through subsequent errors, to the creation of a vapour cloud that was then unwittingly ignited by an idling pick-up truck. John Browne, then BP's Chief Executive, writes 'My blood ran cold' when he heard news of the accident: 'My memory of that day is searing. It was an appalling tragedy.'[9] In the half-decade prior to the disaster, BP had an excellent safety record, but the subsequent Baker Report criticized the company for focusing on occupational safety while neglecting various key aspects of process safety.

The overwhelming majority of industrial accidents are caused by serious mistakes. Sometimes they are made by workers who die or are injured in consequence. More often they are made by managers who are culpable in their choice of equipment and systems, oversee haphazard processes of maintenance and inspection, or fail to create a vigilant safety culture in the company. Workers die as a result.

These incidents leave as their residue a tangled weave of blame, denial and remorse. Bereaved relatives are often consumed with anger; hapless executives are dogged by guilt. Hope is typically in short supply. On the cross, we see Jesus bringing last-ditch encouragement to one of the men crucified with him. This bandit owned up to his own crimes ('we are getting what we deserve for our deeds') in the act of rebuking his colleague who was joining in the derision of Jesus. Jesus in turn brings hope with the startling words, 'Truly I tell you, today you will be with me in Paradise' (Luke 23:43).

The cost of integrity

Companies also die. As with an individual's death in an industrial accident, death can come suddenly and swiftly, though here too retrospective explanations can often be found in terms of decline within the corporate culture. Arthur Andersen, the global accountancy firm fatally implicated in the Enron scandal, is a salutary example.[10] But corporate demise is not necessarily deserved. It is often the experience of a small company that is by definition vulnerable. In a recession, especially, little companies very easily fall foul of circumstances and become the victims of others' manoeuvrings.

The bank may stop lending you money, not because your company is unworthy of credit, but because of a trend that affects the whole banking sector, making lending practice more restrictive. You have a cash-flow problem because customers stop paying you on time, perhaps because their own customers are having difficulty paying *them*. In a financial climate where people are tightening their belts, your own product or service becomes a luxury they can no longer afford. A competitor may be playing dirty tricks on you, vilifying your good name or radically undercutting your company because they can afford to do so. So the difficulties you encounter are not your own fault; you are simply experiencing the harsh facts of life. Nevertheless, the consequences are serious. The threat of death looms over your company.

Practising the qualities commended in this book, notably those of enterprise, passion, prudence and integrity, will frequently bring corporate success. Their deployment offers much hope. But they are no *guarantee* of success. In some lines of business, doing the right thing can be costly. The unwillingness to take moral short cuts may prove critical when margins are tight. Refusing to pay bribes can cost a lot of time and money. Faithfulness may prove sacrificial.

This was the experience of Liz Crowe, the thirty-eight-year-old head of a clinical trials unit with an excellent reputation for high-quality research. The pharmaceutical industry has always had some research of a dubious nature that is more a marketing exercise than a proper clinical trial.

Liz scrupulously avoided such business, so she was seriously concerned when the unit's parent company started to drop its standards and exerted pressure on her to cut corners.

The compromises Liz were expected to make took a variety of forms. One proposal failed to make clear the disease the drug was meant to be treating. Another sought to cut costs by reducing the size of the samples she used in trials. Liz's unhappiness with the parent company came to a head during the process of negotiating a contract with a respectable client which had a dilatory legal department. Liz's practice was never to start trials with patients before a contract had been finalized. The Board of Directors, anxious to keep work moving as fast as possible, told her to make an exception. Liz objected, appealing to the Managing Director with whom she had previously enjoyed an agreeable relationship. 'You will do as you are told!' was his frosty response over the phone.

Liz is a Christian. At the time she was a single parent, recently abandoned by her husband, and had two small children. The consequences of losing her job would be serious. But after going on a sailing holiday to consider her situation and pray about it, she returned with her mind made up. She was not prepared to compromise her standards and jeopardize the reputation of the unit she had painstakingly established. She requested an interview with the Managing Director, who subjected her to a tirade in which he said her scruples were luxuries the parent company could no longer afford. Liz responded by handing in her notice. The company tried to persuade her to stay, but she stood firm.

Resignation was costly for Liz. Most of her savings and ten years of work had been invested in her unit. It was some time before she found a new job that was compatible with her parental responsibilities. But she knew that she must stay true to her integrity, and she experienced a deep peace with God that came from the knowledge that she had done the right thing.

Decisions like Liz's have the character of costly Christlikeness. Resigning on a point of moral principle is not an act to be taken lightly – the attempt should always be made to persuade colleagues to behave differently – but there may come a point when faithful discipleship means taking a costly stand in going it alone. Jesus himself exemplified this.

Self-sacrifice and executive pay

In the case of Jesus, it is clear that, though he was the victim of the hostility and conspiracy of others, he also embraced his fate willingly. He could have attempted to keep out of trouble, keeping a lower profile, being less outspoken in his views and avoiding those dangerous trips to Jerusalem. Instead, he stayed true to his innermost convictions. He accepted a violent end as the price for remaining true to his mission statement and his corporate strapline: bringing good news to the socially marginalized and proclaiming the challenge of the kingdom of God. He would not be deterred, even if that meant sacrificing himself.

Self-sacrifice is a strange concept to discuss in a business context. We are accustomed to thinking that this is one area of life where self-seeking is the name of the game. Since the rise of mainstream economics it is assumed that in the marketplace, individuals and companies single-mindedly pursue their own financial benefit. The best-known passage in *The Wealth of Nations* reads:

> It is not from the benevolence of the butcher, the brewer or the baker that we expect our dinner; but from their regard to their own interest. We address ourselves not to their

humanity but to their self-love, and never talk to them of our own necessities but of their advantage.[11]

Think of two individuals, whether private citizens or car dealers, negotiating the change in ownership of an automobile. We assume that the vendor will try to get as high a price as possible and the buyer will try to pay as little as possible. A deal is struck at the meeting-point between two different parties who are pressing their own interests. This assumption of self-interest is so fundamental that many economists are disconcerted by the suggestion that human beings might act otherwise: it complicates their calculations and – allegedly – distorts the system. This attitude has been gently caricatured in the lyric:

> Maximum utility
> Consumers acting rationally
> They maximise their satisfaction
> And we predict their actions.[12]

With regard to the vexed subject of executive pay, it is often assumed that top executives are maximum utilizers when it comes to their pay package and 'the market' determines how big this is. The laws of supply and demand come into play, and since executive talent is thin on the ground, high salaries are necessary to attract the most talented. Defenders of the status quo see this as an amoral process. If a company fails to pay the going market rate, it won't get the executives it wants.

There is *some* truth in this argument. The salaries paid to those of comparable ability and occupying similar positions undoubtedly influence what individuals expect and demand. We live too in an increasingly mobile world where talent can be attracted from other countries and other business sectors.

The market for executives, however, is far from being the ideal competitive market of economists' dreams. The non-executive directors who set pay tend to be drawn from the same circle of high-earning corporate executives, raising questions about their independence of judgment.

The market also varies a great deal from country to country, even between those of comparable economic stature. Far from being an objective force that operates in a quasi-universal way, the market is subtly yet substantially shaped by the culture in which companies operate. People's attitudes make themselves felt. Sheltering behind the so-called truism that 'the market decides' is self-deceptive. Ultimately, most executive packages are decided by the remuneration sub-committees of boards of directors. They have real choices to make about how much they pay their senior executives, just as the executives do about the packages they choose to accept.

In some countries, high levels of executive pay are seen as damaging society. Luxembourg Prime Minister Jean-Claude Junker described them as 'a social scourge':[13] huge pay packets and massive differentials create a rift between people. They affect national and corporate morale; they exacerbate social divisions. Those at the lower end of the wage spectrum feel demoralized and underappreciated. Those at the higher end become objects of envy and resentment.

The negative social results of this are documented in *The Spirit Level*, where Richard Wilkinson and Kate Pickett draw on around 200 different sets of data from reputable sources such as the United Nations, the World Bank and the World Health Organization. They show that on almost every index of quality of life, happiness or deprivation, a strong correlation exists between a country's level of economic inequality and its social outcomes. So countries with extreme inequality like the UK and the USA score poorly on indices such as mental

health, obesity, crime and longevity, in contrast to more egalitarian countries such as Sweden and Japan. The countries lying
somewhere in between economically, like Australia and
Germany, also occupy the middle ground socially.[14]

The alleged necessity of paying large salaries to attract the
best people also begs questions about personal motivation.
The view that markets operate amorally makes three questionable assumptions: that people are motivated by self-interest;
that self-interest is not a matter of morality; and that self-
interest consists essentially in a calculation of financial benefits.
Clearly, the lure of money is a strong motivating factor for
many. But human beings are too varied, too interesting and
too concerned about other people for this view of *homo
economicus* to convince as a universal description.[15] Senior
executives may be motivated to work hard and serve their
company well for a whole variety of reasons including self-
respect, job satisfaction, intellectual stimulus, innate creativity,
leadership drive, joy in teamwork, a congenial working
environment, meeting a challenge and a spur to excellence.

In the case of many highly paid executives, their affluence
is such that the presence or absence of, say, an additional
half-million in their pay package is unlikely to make much
difference either to their lifestyle or their work-rate. They
might agree with the former chief executive of Shell, Jeroen
van der Veer, who said: 'You have to realise: if I had been
paid 50 per cent more, I would not have done it better. If I
had been paid 50 per cent less, then I would not have done
it worse.'[16]

Assessing motivation is further complicated by the fact
that remuneration packages are precisely that – packages. As
well as basic salary, remuneration may consist of short-term
bonuses, long-term incentive plans, share options, compensation arrangements, and perks such as company cars and

country club membership. These 'extras' can easily end up doubling or tripling a basic salary. The level of take-home pay is also affected by the amount of tax paid. That can vary greatly both between countries and within countries, depending on the rate of taxation, the nature of the package and the advice of an executive's accountant. Such complexity gives rise to another objection, the frequent lack of clarity about a package's total value and how it is calculated. So there are cries for greater transparency and fuller public disclosure in executive remuneration. The more complicated the package, the harder it is for outsiders to ascertain the full value of what executives are being paid.

Executive pay, then, is an area that exhibits more variety and gives more scope for personal choice than is often claimed. Individuals can choose *not* to be maximum utilizers. They can settle for less than the 'going rate' in their particular business sector. In chapter 6 we saw how bankers currently find themselves in a peculiarly delicate situation, because their actions (as a group) played a significant role in triggering the global financial crisis and necessitating the cutbacks that bring hardship to many. This was a point lost on Bob Diamond, the American Chief Executive of Barclays Bank, when he defended the reintroduction of big bonus payments by banks before a Treasury Select Committee of MPs in January 2011. He said, 'there was a period of remorse and apology for banks and I think that period needs to be over.'[17]

But surely collective self-restraint continues to be appropriate in a climate where public sector workers are receiving redundancy notices and pension reductions. A St Paul's Institute report into the attitudes of finance sector professionals in the City of London revealed that while 64% of participants thought salary and bonuses were the most important factors that motivated them, most also thought that they were paid too much and 75% that the gap between rich and poor is too great. Personal gain, peer pressure and loyalty to colleagues are actually at odds with what many bankers and brokers deep down believe. Could Christians in that sector set a courageous example in helping people be true to their convictions and – like Stephen Hester, Chief Executive of RBS – forego the bonuses awarded to them?

Self-sacrifice and fair trade

Self-denial can also be practised as we make purchases. The fair trade movement revolves around customers choosing to pay more than they need to, buying goods they could get more cheaply. According to the maximum utility theory, this again appears irrational. An economist's explanation for such behaviour is that 'the consumers' utility preference function includes a supplementary type of utility in addition to the functional utility from the consumption of the good'.[18] This is gobbledegook. Customers buy fair trade products because they want to help poor producers in the developing world.

Fair trade is still a tiny proportion of overall global trade, but it is growing fast. Worldwide sales increased over the last decade by an average 40% each year to a figure of £2.5 billion in 2010. In the UK, retail sales were £1.2 million, among which coffee accounted for £157m and bananas £209m.[19] Since 2008 Sainsbury's and Waitrose have stocked fair trade bananas exclusively, while Starbucks sells only fair trade coffee in its UK restaurants. The Fairtrade Foundation calculates that over seven million people (producers, their families and communities) in sixty developing countries are benefiting from fair trade. Fair trade markets exist in twenty-three countries, mainly the relatively affluent countries of Europe and North America, but now include some developing countries like India.

Fair trade organizations like Traidcraft seek to improve the livelihood and wellbeing of producers in four interrelated ways, as follows.

Improving market access

This includes finding a market for goods and selling them, as well as suggesting how to improve products. The quality needs to be high and the product something that people genuinely want. Fair trade coffee that tastes foul is no longer tolerated! Indeed, it is increasingly a thing of the past – many excellent fair trade coffees are available. By making some of the purchases in advance, fair trade organizations also provide valuable credit.

Strengthening producers' organizations

Producers are helped to learn new skills and develop new techniques. The participation of women is encouraged and when children are used in the production process, they are protected from exploitation. Environmental sustainability is a requirement.

Paying a better price

The price covers the full cost of production and enables workers to be paid whatever constitutes a living wage in their context. Fair trade certification guarantees a stable minimum price even when the global market price for the commodity falls. In addition, a social premium – usually an extra 10% – is paid for producers to invest in business development, social and developmental projects.

Providing continuity in the trading relationship

Traidcraft enters into long-term relationships with producers, so there is some assurance of repeat orders. Partnership entails working with producers to rectify mistakes and overcome problems. However, long-term doesn't necessarily mean 'for ever'. A fair trade company may become strong enough not to need continuing assistance.

Fair trade inspection and certification are carried out by the Fairtrade Labelling Organization (FLO), an independent body which ensures that both producers and traders comply with internationally agreed standards.

On the surface, fair trade looks like an undiluted success story, with many major supermarkets now selling products carrying the Fairtrade Mark, high-public recognition of the logo and sales expected to continue growing. The price of this success, however, is that the movement is being exposed to some serious questions. These warrant careful consideration.

1. Does fair trade actually make individuals better off?
Scepticism has been expressed about this, since wholesalers and retailers take some of the mark-up. Also, though a minimum price may be guaranteed, the quantity of goods bought from the producers is not guaranteed; fair trade is still subject to market variables. In reality, many fair trade producers sell a considerable share of their produce on conventional markets. The research evidence is patchy, but the indications are that measured by money in their pockets, these producers may be only slightly better off than their peers.[20] What is undeniably true are the benefits brought by the wise use of social premiums to the cooperatives or communities of which they are a part. In Chile, Apicoop has used premiums mainly for business development, such as the purchase of fork-lift trucks; Lautaro has invested in education, so that producers' children are now able to attend university for the first time. In other parts of the world,

producers have ploughed the money into wells, schools and health clinics, all of which bring palpable community benefits.

2. Aren't the costs of participating in fair trade unreasonably high?

A producers' organization may operate according to fair trade standards, but find the cost of initial certification prohibitively expensive: FLO–CERT charges £1,570 for an initial inspection and certification, and £145 for subsequent recertification.[21] These are huge sums for a fledgling organization, and help explain why fair trade has so far made limited impact in the poorest countries. In Nairobi I visited Safaribead, a crafts manufacturer employing about fifteen Maasai women. It was founded by Lisa Barratt, who emigrated north after being evicted with her husband from their farm in Zimbabwe by Mugabe's soldiers in 2002. Safaribead do a good line in beaded sandals and ingenious recycling, turning discarded flip-flops into toy animals and cars. But though a member of the international Ethical Fashion Forum, Safaribead lacked the fair trade label because their cash-flow didn't stretch to the cost of certification. It is encouraging that the Fairtrade Foundation has now set up a Producer Certification Fund whereby organizations can apply for a grant covering up to 75% of their fee. Some groups also receive help in paying fees from their commercial partners.

3. Doesn't the involvement of big supermarkets and chains threaten the integrity of the fair trade movement?

The argument runs that fair trade began as an 'alternative' business model, but nothing could be less alternative than Tesco or Asda, which now stock fair trade products. How can we be sure that big business won't dilute fair trade standards, since they lack any strong ideological commitment to the movement and view fair trade as one niche market among others? This is a valid concern. It is here that certifying bodies prove their worth, because they guarantee the legitimacy of all products bearing the Mark.

Fairtrade Foundation Director Harriet Lamb has also identified some genuine fair trade enthusiasts at senior levels in big companies.[22] The Cooperative Group, now the fifth largest supermarket in the UK, belongs in a special category: its commitment is unequivocal and it carries a much wider range of fair trade products than its competitors. 'Mainstream' selling through the supermarkets certainly expands awareness of fair trade products and boosts their sales.

4. Does fair trade encourage over-production?

Economists tend to surmise that, since producers are protected (to some extent) from market fluctuations, they are inclined to produce more than they can sell. This has a damaging effect on the market as a whole, the fall in overall prices driving farmers who aren't in fair trade arrangements into more extreme poverty. Although the economic theory sounds plausible, empirical research has failed to confirm it. The Institute of Economic Affairs takes a critical attitude towards fair trade, but their recent report *Fair Trade Without the Froth* found no evidence of this distorting negative effect. It concluded that such problems are unlikely to be substantial as long as fair trade remains a relatively small player in the market as a whole.[23] In addition, some fair trade farmers, far from over-producing, are diversifying. Apicoop recently bought a thirty-seven-acre field where it grows blueberries to supplement its main produce of honey.

Fair trade is not a universal panacea. There are other ways to alleviate poverty, as China is proving; fair trade is not yet a reality there. The widespread use of mobile phones is proving a significant boost to entrepreneurial activity in Africa. But my involvement in Traidcraft as a Foundation Trustee and my visits to fair trade producers in three different continents convince me that it plays a valuable role. It is a sign of hope, a vehicle for people to provide mutual support, within developing countries and across continents. It is also a movement in which Christians have made a prominent pioneering contribution.

The testimony of Purity Muthoni, a Kenyan tea grower, is typical of many fair trade producers. 'Tea helps me in many ways: to educate, to provide the family with food, good clothes, buying cows. Because of Fairtrade our lives are improved.' Now Purity has fresh water to make tea because she and her husband, William, have used money from their tea sales to build a well next to their house.

The self-sacrifice entailed in making a fair trade purchase may appear so slight as to be scarcely worthy of the name. But the cost can be genuine. Where the effort is made to buy fair trade regularly and extensively, significant outlay is involved. When times are hard and income reduced, it is tempting to forget others in far-off lands whose needs are much greater than ours. Inspired by the love of Christ, let us stiffen our resolve to prove that we do not automatically have to buy cheap.

The toxic handler

An article in the *Harvard Business Review* draws attention to the role played in many organizations by what the authors call *toxic handlers*.[24] They are individuals who absorb and soften emotional pain, voluntarily shouldering the sadness, frustration, bitterness and anger that are endemic to corporate life. They often soak up flak from a variety of directions.

Sometimes a toxic handler is the chief executive's front man, 'translating his seemingly irrational directives so that people could put them into action'.[25] They listen empathetically, suggest solutions, work behind the scenes, carry the confidences of others and reframe difficult messages. Although toxic handlers save organizations from self-destructing, they often pay a steep price – professionally, psychologically and sometimes physically.

I certainly know some Christians who play this type of corporate role. In doing so, they usually look for inspiration from one who absorbed no limits of poisonous bile when he was crucified. This doesn't make being a toxic handler easy, but it can make it endurable. I have already cited one of Jesus' words from the cross – his message of hope to a convicted criminal. In testing circumstances at work, we do well to reflect on his other memorable sayings.

First, Jesus shows awareness of and concern for others despite the excruciating pain he was suffering. He sees his mother and best friend standing by the cross and commends them to each other's care: 'Woman, here is your son' and 'Here is your mother' (John 19:26–27).

Second, Jesus speaks and breathes forgiveness. 'Father, forgive them; for they do not know what they are doing' (Luke 23:34). At work, we often encounter people who give us grief: they annoy us intensely, attack us incessantly or undermine our exploits. Such 'enemies' may include people we are trying to help. Allan Bussard, a Canadian social entrepreneur who set up a fair trade macadamia nut factory in Kenya, was rewarded for his efforts by workers stealing nuts and, when he moved location, by sabotaging the second factory through blowing up a boiler.[26] Stress, anger and bitterness can easily build up in a business environment. Jesus' response is to pray ('Father') and to take the positive response of forgiving, not seeking revenge. Bussard has refused to abandon his enterprise in Kenya and, after two false starts, appears to have found a more cooperative workforce.

Third, Jesus does not hide his humanity behind a veneer of religiosity. True to the experience of any crucified man, he is desperately thirsty and says so (John 19:28). Moreover, though he goes to the cross believing this was God's will for him, he experiences the agony of abandonment; echoing Psalm 22, he cries from his personal darkness, 'My God, my God, why have you forsaken me?' (Mark 15:34). When Christians don't understand what God is up to, it is best to be honest. Sometimes we witness to others most effectively when we allow them into our doubts and questionings, making exploration of faith a shared experience rather than pretending we have all the answers.

Fourth, Jesus is a completer-finisher. The episode of God-forsakenness seems to have passed, because Jesus' stint on the cross ends with two sentences that express the sense of a job well done. 'Father, into your hands I commend my spirit' (Luke 23:46); 'It is finished' (John 19:30). Jesus was able to commit himself and the work he had done to the Father God who had sustained him through it.

Resurrection: confirmed and vindicated

Jesus' disciples were devastated when he died. Their dreams and hopes for a liberated Israel lay in ruins. The charismatic, enigmatic master they had accompanied for three years was gone, leaving a huge void. It is clear from the Gospel accounts that the resurrection of Jesus took them completely by surprise.

This is especially evident in the account of the two lesser-known disciples walking home to the village of Emmaus (Luke 24:13–35). Cleopas and his companion – possibly his wife – are absorbed in gloomy discussion about the tragic fate that has befallen their leader. Their heads are down, their spirits at rock bottom. Even when the risen Jesus joins them and talks with them, they fail to recognize him. True, a profound experience is taking place. The couple express this later by saying, 'Were not our hearts burning within us while he was talking to us on the road, while he was opening the scriptures to us?' (Luke 24:32). This suggests a gradually increasing understanding, a slowly dawning recognition, perhaps even a warmth blossoming into love for this mysterious interpreter.

But it is only after they invite him in and through Jesus' characteristic act of breaking bread that the penny drops. Cleopas and his companion realize who Jesus is. The effect is electrifying.[27] Forgetting the weariness of their seven-mile walk, they leap from their chairs and hurry back to Jerusalem to tell the other disciples. It turns out that this was not Jesus' first resurrection appearance, nor his last, prompting the disciples' excited acclamation: 'the Lord has risen indeed!' (Luke 24:34).

Jesus' resurrection was God's way of confirming his unique identity. Otherwise we would have no reason to accord Jesus anything more than a minor footnote in history, an eccentric, itinerant Jewish rabbi who came to a sadly sticky end. The resurrection gives sold ground for endorsing the confession made by the Roman centurion at the cross: 'Truly this man was God's Son! (Mark 15:39). In Romans 1:4 Paul says Jesus 'was declared to be the Son of God with power according to the spirit of holiness by resurrection from the dead' – a key part of the gospel. We have seen how the question of Jesus' identity caused controversy throughout his ministry. By raising him from the dead, God supplied the answer. The breathtaking power inherent in the act was God's way of proclaiming that Jesus was indeed part of his being, a man who could rightly be styled *Son of God*.

Furthermore, Jesus is *vindicated* by his resurrection. It was God's stamp of approval, not just on the person of Jesus, but on the mission he came to perform. The resurrection gives us reason for regarding the cross not as a tragedy (though it certainly contained a tragic dimension), but as falling within God's purposes. This brings us back to the question with which this chapter began: why did Jesus die? Along with the human explanation lies a divine explanation. As the followers of Jesus reviewed what had happened, recalled things he had said and re-read certain Old Testament passages, they came to understand Jesus' death as God's way of saving the world. They spelled this out in a theology of atonement: God and humanity made-at-one.

Cancelling the IOU

There is no one definitive explanation of how the cross secures our salvation in the New Testament. The meaning of Jesus' death is explained in several places, by Jesus himself, Peter, Hebrews, John and above all Paul. But a variety of phraseology is used. Jesus uses the language of hostage release in saying that the Son of Man came 'to give his life as a ransom for many' (Matthew 10:4; cf. Revelation 5:9). Peter says that Jesus 'bore our sins in his body on the cross' (1 Peter 2:24), Hebrews that Christ 'offered for all time a single sacrifice for sins' (Hebrews 10:12), John that he is the 'propitiation' for our sins (1 John 2:2).[28] Paul also uses the word propitiation (by Christ's blood) in Romans 3:25, but links this with the concepts of justification and redemption, an interesting combination of metaphors from the temple precincts, law courts and marketplace. Elsewhere he uses the ideas of reconciliation (Colossians 1:20; 2 Corinthians 5:19), foolishness

(1 Corinthians 1:18) and victory over the forces of evil (Colossians 2:15).

It is mistaken to drive a wedge between these different images, as some theologians have done, opting for one theory of atonement to the exclusion of others.[29] The images are complementary rather than contradictory, and considerable areas of overlap exist between them. All agree that the cross dealt conclusively with the problem of human sin; all agree that Jesus died in our stead or on our behalf. He took the full weight of sin upon himself, and made possible a new restored relationship with God.

The New Testament simply provides us with a range of pictures illustrating how this happened: helpfully, because some capture people's imagination more than others. Moreover, effective communication relates to historical and geographical context. Christians in every generation need to ask which biblical metaphors speak most vividly to their own society. In a world where debt is such a massive problem, and underlay the recent financial crisis, the image of sin as *debt* is peculiarly powerful.

This metaphor existed in the Aramaic language that Jesus spoke. Most versions of the Lord's Prayer follow Luke's version, which says 'Forgive us our sins', but Matthew's version uses a different word that is probably closer to the original: 'forgive us our debts, as we also have forgiven our debtors' (Matthew 6:12). The German *Schuld* likewise means both debt and guilt. Our sins, which comprise a repeated breaking of God's law, create an overdraft: failing to honour God as we should, we are in debt to him.

Paul picks up this metaphor in Colossians 2:13–14: 'And when you were dead in trespasses and the uncircumcision of your flesh, God made you alive together with Christ, when he forgave us all our trespasses, erasing the record that stood against us with its legal demands.' The Greek word *cheirographon*, translated 'record' in the NRSV and more often 'bond' (RSV, NIV) signifies a handwritten note or certificate of indebtedness – an IOU. Paul says God 'set this aside, nailing it to the cross' (Colossians 2:14). Normally a tablet detailing a crucified man's crimes was fixed over his head.[30] Paul pictures our catalogue of sins being inscribed above the cross of Jesus: he paid humanity's collective IOU. It was probably this immense burden of debt weighing on him so heavily that caused Jesus to feel forsaken by God on the cross. But the effect was liberating. God cancelled the IOU: 'erasing' means 'wiped away'. All record of our debt was removed. This way of understanding has a special relevance for our debt-ridden societies as Christians seek to explain the cross today.

A living hope

Paul says God 'made you alive', together with Christ. Death and resurrection are not things that just happened to Jesus; they can happen to us too. Peter waxes lyrical about the hope this generates:

> Blessed be the God and Father of our Lord Jesus Christ! By his great mercy he has give us a new birth into a living hope through the resurrection of Jesus Christ from the dead, and into an inheritance that is imperishable, undefiled, and unfading, kept in heaven for you . . .
> (1 Peter 1:3–4).

Jesus' resurrection provides sure ground for hope that we, like him, will experience life beyond the grave. But the new life actually starts *now*, this side of death. Paul speaks of baptism as signifying this transition. We die to sin as we 'drown' in the water and then resurface to a life freed from the penalty and power of sin: ' . . . we have been buried with him by baptism into death, so that just as Christ was raised from the dead by the glory of the Father, so we too might walk in newness of life' (Romans 6:4).

If we take this new, living reality seriously, what might the resurrection mean for the world of business? Are there prospects for a radical new start *there* and, if so, what might they look like? If companies and careers can die, can they also be resurrected? Here we are dependent on God's stirring. The disciples' words from the Emmaus road, 'Did not our hearts burn within us?', are strangely apt. For resurrection in business terms to happen, recognition and understanding of what occurred in the past is necessary. How and why have I or we reached our present position? What has God been doing and what is God now saying?

Jesus' death and resurrection matter first and foremost because through these momentous events God acted for our salvation. But it takes nothing away from their uniqueness to say that they also mirror something going on more widely in God's world. Jesus saw this when, in relation to his glorification on the cross, he said: 'I tell you the truth, unless a grain of wheat falls into the earth and dies, it remains just a single grain; but if it dies, it bears much fruit' (John 12:24). C. S. Lewis observed of such processes that 'The pattern is there in nature because it was first there in God'.[31] We see many examples of the divine theme of death and rebirth in what Lewis calls a 'minor key'. They occur in the organizational world as well as in nature.

Transformation: different types of company

When Jesus rose from the dead, his body was transformed. It was the same but different: there was sufficient continuity that the disciples could see and feel the wounds in his side

(John 20:24–29), and enough discontinuity that he was no longer subject to the same restraints and could now pass through locked doors (John 20:19). Paul promises a similar blend for us: the resurrection body is sown physical and raised spiritual (1 Corinthians 15:44). Transformation signifies a condition that is very different – gloriously so – but not completely different.

Let us apply this idea to a business context. Christians who have experienced corporate failure may, having taken advice and prayed fervently, feel that God is calling them to make a new start. Hopefully a new company will not just be more of the same, an old business resuscitated and given a fresh name. Rather, a transformed business is one raised to a new level or quality. Novelty may be apparent in improved products, new niche markets, diversified offerings or quality of management. But it may also be appropriate to think of a different sort of company with an alternative *structure*.

The corporate structure that dominates global capitalism is the public limited company (PLC). In Britain, the 1862 Companies Act, which consolidated earlier legislation, enshrined the principle of limited liability for shareholders. Companies had found that once they reached a certain stage, they could only secure the infusion of capital required for further expansion if the risk entailed was substantially reduced. Limiting liability to shareholders' original stake in the firm meant that they could buy shares unfettered by fears of paying out large sums if the firm failed. This way of structuring firms has proved very effective in terms of raising capital, especially for companies operating globally.

However, limited liability is strongly criticized for several reasons. It has produced a system where – to use Michael Schluter's language – a vast relational distance exists between capital provider and user. Providers of capital generally have little or no say in corporate decision-making. Many members of the public buy shares through a financial intermediary, such as a pension fund; 'often they do not even know (or care) in which companies they hold shares.'[32] They seldom attend the company's annual general meeting. Even the institutional shareholders rarely influence corporate policy, opting to 'exit' if things go badly rather than offering constructive advice to the management. They tend to judge companies simply by the yardstick of their latest quarterly financial results. In addition, limited liability can mean that creditors such as suppliers are left unpaid if a company goes bankrupt, imperilling their own future prospects.

From a Christian perspective, the ideal form of organization is one where every member has a distinct role, knows the other members and appreciates their contribution. St Paul talks about the church as Christ's body in this vein (1 Corinthians 12:3–30; cf. Romans 12:4–8). While the Corinthian context was the need to avoid damaging church splits between those with different gifts by stressing their interdependence, the model has obvious relevance to any organization involving human cooperation. Shareholders in PLCs make a significant contribution, but their *modus operandi* is typically hands-off and devoid of real relationship with other corporate stakeholders.

There are genuine alternatives to PLCs. Britain's private companies include some major names in retailing, construction and utilities. A leading place is occupied by the John Lewis Partnership, which operates twenty-nine department stores, 274 Waitrose supermarkets and six At Home stores. It has a fascinating history.

In 1864, Somerset-born John Lewis opened a drapery shop on Oxford Street, and by 1895 had expanded this to create a department store selling a wide variety of goods. He did this entirely from retained profits; by living frugally he saved enough to finance each new step without needing to bring in investors or form a joint stock company. The whole store belonged to him alone, and he ran it autocratically. His son John Spedan Lewis followed him into the business but became increasingly critical of his father's approach. In particular, he was shocked to realize that he, his brother and his father were raking in a sum equal to the entire wage bill for the 300 employees. 'Why should the employers claim the whole or almost the whole of the profit?' he asked. His father was unimpressed but allowed Spedan to run a second store, Peter Jones, where he introduced democratic practices, shorter hours and longer holidays, but still returned handsome profits that he shared among the employees. When Lewis senior died in 1928, Spedan took total control of the business, which he then 'resurrected' as a different sort of company: a partnership comprising an irrevocable trust settlement that turned ownership over to the company's employees. Employees remain full partners in John Lewis. Spedan devised an elaborate constitution to ensure that all were represented in decision-making processes, while giving the board of directors full power to manage the business on their behalf.

You can listen to Spedan, then aged seventy, propounding his radical ideas in splendidly statesmanlike style on the company website.[33] 'The present state of affairs is a perversion of the proper workings of capitalism'; 'it is all wrong to have millionaires before you have ceased to have slums'; 'there must be some inequalities but they should be the least possible'; 'partnership for all should take the place of exploitation'.

Today John Lewis sets a limit on pay differentials; the highest paid is only allowed to earn seventy-five times the lowest.[34] That is still a handsome salary but it contrasts with a ratio of 750:1 at Tesco, where the total salary package of former chief executive Sir Terry Leahy added up to over £9m. Yet John Lewis has more than matched Tesco's success in recent years, coming through the recession impressively. Moreover, ordinary employees as well as directors benefit from bonuses when profits are high.[35] No wonder that one is almost always assured of friendly helpful service when shopping in John Lewis.

Variations on the partnership model abound. The UK Cooperative Group allows customers to become members, using a card when they make a purchase and receiving a profit share biannually. The world's largest cooperative, the Mondragon Corporation in the Basque area of Spain, has 85,000 worker-owners. It weathered the 2009 slump in machine tools and car components by putting 20% of staff (chosen by lottery) on leave for a year at 80% of their pay. All new workers put up 13,400 euros in share capital. The system is run by an elected Congress, known as 'the supreme expression of sovereignty'.

Mondragon was founded by a Catholic priest, José Maria Arizmendiarrieta, to relieve parishioners from the devastation left by the Spanish Civil War. Current chairman José Maria Aldecoa makes no pretence that Mondragon is perfect. 'The cooperative model is absolutely flawed,' he admits disarmingly, 'but it has shown itself the least flawed in a crisis of values and models.'[36]

Once a company has adopted a particular corporate structure, it is not easy to change it – but far from impossible. If employees have access to sufficient capital, they may be able to buy out the shareholders. The Baxi Partnership, itself an employee-owned company, runs a £20m fund aimed at facilitating employee buy-outs in the UK and a consultancy which helps employee-owned companies develop a genuine partnership culture.[37] David Erdal, author of *Beyond the Corporation*, describes several firms that have prospered from the resulting increased levels of employee enthusiasm and commitment. Companies can be reborn. As such they constitute a real sign of hope in the global economy.

Micro-credit

Mention has already been made of micro-finance and its targeting of loans towards women in the developing world. We have seen how the main thrust of the Old Testament prohibition on usury concerns the treatment of the poor and protection against their being exploited. An innovative type of banking that makes loans available to the world's poor and claims to have their best interests at heart therefore warrants close attention.

The best-known bank to specialize in micro-credit is the Grameen Bank. It was the brainchild of Muhammad Yunus when a youthful Professor of Economics in his home city of Chittagong, Bangladesh. In 1974, Yunus launched a research project into rural poverty in the nearby village of Jobra, having decided that 'I would become a student all over again, and Jobra would be my university. The people of Jobra would be my teachers'.[38] He discovered how loan sharks had effectively enslaved the villagers. Motivated to get practically involved, he started to lend money in the village himself. What was originally called the Grameen Bank Project ('Grameen' means 'rural' in Bengali) became an independent bank in 1983. Its capital comes from a combination of donations, loans from the central bank of Bangladesh, bond sales and savers' deposits.

The Grameen Bank is largely owned by the 8.3 million Bangladeshi women – spread across 80,000 villages – it predominantly seeks to serve. In a workshop involving 100 of these women in 1984, the Bank adopted Sixteen Decisions that are regularly recited both by bank employees and the five-member groups to whom loans are made. These decisions include commitments not to live in dilapidated houses, to grow vegetables and sell the surplus, to use pit-latrines, to drink water from wells and to educate their children. The underlying ethos is expressed in Commitment 14: 'We shall always be ready to help each other. If anyone is in difficulty, we shall all help him or her.'[39]

In the Grameen Bank's system of solidarity lending, repayment responsibility rests squarely on the individual borrower, but the group of which she is part exercises oversight, ensuring that everyone behaves responsibly. The Bank claims repayment rates as high as 98%. The fact that it instils discipline by requiring repayment in small weekly instalments from the onset of the loan contributes to this success. In 2006, the Nobel Prize for Peace was awarded jointly to Muhammad Yunus and the Grameen Bank 'for their efforts to create economic and social development from below'.[40]

Although Yunus is often described as the founder of micro-credit, that is not strictly true. Several Christian organizations have been involved in micro-finance since the 1970s, including Opportunity International, which was founded in 1971 by American Al Whittaker and Australian David Bussau.[41] It serves over 2 million clients in more than twenty countries. Opportunity International is notable for its pioneering advance of electronic and mobile technology to reduce transaction costs and bring banking services to the most marginalized and remote peoples.

Through its subsidiary, MicroEnsure, it also provides protection against the many risks faced by those living in poverty. With average premiums of about $1.50 per month for a family of five, MicroEnsure is making life insurance affordable to many for the first time in Ghana, Kenya, India, the Philippines and Tanzania.[42]

The microfinance charity Five Talents was founded at the Lambeth Conference of Anglican Church leaders in 1998 as 'a long-term response to help the poor in developing countries based on need, not creed'.[43] Five Talents provides small loans to groups of entrepreneurs, using a similar model to the Grameen Bank, as well as offering business training and mentoring. Its 'Business as Mission' programme coordinates short-term mission trips and the teaching of a biblically based curriculum that covers the basics of entrepreneurship, business planning, marketing and record-keeping. It incorporates case studies and interactive exercises that do not depend on intimidating standards of literacy.[44] Active in eleven developing countries and with a repayment rate of 95%, Five Talents is attracting increasing recognition for its work, having won several sustainable business awards.

While visiting Bangalore in July 2010, I met the dynamic Collin Timms, a self-made businessman who became rich by the age of thirty but yearned for a different goal in life. A priest asked him to help someone struggling in business. The satisfaction he experienced in doing this inspired him with a wider desire to serve others. He is now managing trustee of the Bridge Foundation, an Indian micro-credit organization which is affiliated to Opportunity International; it seeks to provide a 'bridge' from need to opportunity. The Foundation has helped start about 140,000 small-scale enterprises in five south Indian states. Timms says, 'Our clients are typically village shop owners or tiny dairies where women own one or two cows. Often a short-term loan of $150 is enough to get them started.' The Bridge Foundation has made a particular effort to stimulate micro-enterprises among families where the chief breadwinner has gone to prison.[45] Timms is a man motivated by a vision for channelling money in productive directions to bring about social change.

Sadly, micro-finance is under a cloud at the time of writing. The centre of controversy is one of the states in which the Bridge Foundation operates, Andhra Pradesh, where a rash of client suicides (allegedly thirty within a couple of months in late 2010) has been blamed on the heavy techniques to exact payments being used by micro-finance institutions.[46] What appears to have happened is that unscrupulous commercial micro-finance institutions that lack a strong ideological commitment to clients' welfare have got in on the act. A movement intended to replace loan sharks has, in turn, been penetrated by loan sharks. Such is the fallen state of humanity that no business sector is unaffected.

In response, the Andhra Pradesh Government has curtailed the activities of micro-finance organizations. The same impulse for Government control is evident in Bangladesh, whose Government is seeking to increase its ownership stake in the Grameen Bank (claiming that village women are not competent to run it) and Muhammad Yunus resigned as Managing Director in May 2011.[47]

However, the criticisms of micro-credit go deeper than this. The charge of usury in the sense of exorbitant interest has been levelled against the industry as a whole, including the Grameen Bank, which typically charges annual rates of about 20%. (Five Talents' average rate is 2.5% per month.)[48] In the light of Exodus 22 and Leviticus 25, the initial Christian response may be to regard *any* charging of interest to the poor as reprehensible. But such a position is unrealistic. Interest-free loans may be practical for personal loans on a one-to-one basis, but once an organization is created to handle the process of lending, costs accumulate. Loan officers who collect money and give advice need to be paid: they are 'worthy of their hire' (Luke 10:7). The Grameen Bank now employs more than 20,000 people. Even in an efficiently run, altruistically motivated, not-for-profit micro-finance organization, charging interest is necessary to cover the costs of the operation and ensure sustainability.

Nevertheless, the level of interest rates is a matter of concern, and micro-finance organizations need to be vigilant that they – like the money-lenders before and around them – do not end up trapping poor people in a cycle of constant repayments. Perhaps there needs to be a shift of emphasis in terms of encouraging savings as much as loans.[49] The former has always been a significant part of the micro-finance movement, but it lacks the glamour and profitability of lending. Yet the gradual build-up of savings may offer a better long-term hope of people's release from a cycle of dependence to become self-sufficient.

The micro-finance movement, to which Christians have made a sterling contribution, has grown fast and there are now a myriad of players. Christian micro-finance organizations need to lead the way in refocusing the sector on helping the poor become economically active. That would be a resurrection of sorts. Micro-finance is not the whole answer to the alleviation of poverty, but it is an important piece of the jigsaw.

An irrepressible spirit

In his speech at Pentecost, the apostle Peter says of Jesus: 'God raised him up, having freed him from death, because it was impossible for him to be held in its power' (Acts 2:24). A premature death could not contain Jesus; his spirit was irrepressible. Hope that springs from the resurrection leads to that same irrepressibility of spirit. This is relevant both to the ability to recover from setbacks in business and to the capacity to spawn fresh ideas. 'If anyone is in Christ, there is a new creation' (2 Corinthians 5:17): a statement with implications for work on Monday as much as church on Sunday.

This verse is an inspiration for Ashish Raichur, a pastor-businessman whom I met in Bangalore. In January 2001 he set up New Creation Information Technologies, a software company with twenty employees, specializing in healthcare for external markets in Canada, the USA, South America and the Middle East. In February 2001 he set up All Peoples Church, which has three congregations in the city and eight church plants outside Bangalore. He has no doubt that God called him to both ministries. Remarkably, Ashish runs both church and company from the same office. I watched in open-mouthed astonishment as he moved effortlessly with a minimum of fuss from giving instructions to his church secretary to discussing a software problem with an engineer. No sacred–secular divide here! His company bears the name it does because he wanted to demonstrate the new creation in business. The evidence is that, in the power of the Holy Spirit, he is doing precisely that.

8. A PEOPLE OF HOPE: ENTERPRISING MONKS AND CARING EMPLOYERS

The day of Pentecost is truly described as the birthday of the Christian Church. After Jesus' resurrection and just before his ascension, he told his disciples that 'you will receive power when the Holy Spirit has come upon you; and you will be my witnesses in Jerusalem, and all Judea and Samaria, and to the ends of the earth' (Acts 1:8). This empowerment was spectacular. The coming of the Spirit gave Jesus' followers a startling ability to speak other languages, enabling them to communicate 'God's deeds of power' in the native tongues of the Jewish pilgrims present in Jerusalem for the feast of Pentecost.

The Spirit also released them from the fear that had marked their behaviour prior to Jesus' death. Thus Peter, who had denied even that he knew Jesus, boldly addressed the gathering crowd, proclaiming that God had raised up the Jesus whom 'you crucified and killed by the hands of those outside the law' (Acts 2:23–24). When the Jewish religious authorities (understandably angered by such talk) arrested him and John, Peter – 'filled with the Holy Spirit' – surprised them with a splendidly lucid speech (Acts 4:8–13).

The impact of Pentecost was remarkable. Three thousand people responded to Peter's message. They were baptized, and 'devoted themselves to the apostles' teaching and fellowship, to the breaking of bread and prayers' (Acts 2:42). A radical experiment in egalitarian living followed: having all things in common, they sold their possessions and goods, distributing the proceeds to any in need – exemplified by Barnabas, who gave the money from the sale of a field to the apostles for distribution to needy members of the new community (Acts 4:32–37).

Initially this community was entirely Jewish. But three factors impelled them to move outwards. First, persecution had a scattering, centrifugal effect (Acts 8:1). Second, Jesus had told the disciples to go and 'make disciples of all nations' (Matthew 28:19). Third, it was only natural that, in grasping the full significance of Jesus' death and resurrection – that God was 'in Christ, reconciling the world to himself' (2 Corinthians 5:19) – they wanted to share this message with humanity at large. Paul saw reconciliation both on a horizontal level, between human beings, and on a vertical level, between humanity and God. Christ had broken down the barrier between Jew and Gentile (Ephesians 2:11–16), and God's purpose was that Gentiles 'become fellow-heirs, members of the same body, and sharers in the promise in Christ Jesus through the gospel' (Ephesians 3:6). God's hope for humanity had resumed its universal orientation. Because the believers held that Jesus was the promised Messiah (Greek *Christos*), they were nicknamed Christians (Acts 11:26). The word 'church', meanwhile, expressed their identity as a group 'called out' (Greek *ecclesia*) to be in fellowship with each other and conformed to the image of Christ (Romans 8:28–29; 1 Corinthians 1:2–9).

The early Christians were passionate about spreading the good news of salvation. This was their major preoccupation. At the same time they needed to sustain themselves economically. Paul's trade was tent-making, and while in Corinth he stayed and worked with Priscilla and Aquila, a converted couple who were also tent-makers (Acts 18:1–3). His main interest, though, lay in seeking to persuade the Jews and Greeks whom he encountered weekly in the synagogue (18:4). Paul felt justified in expecting the church to support him, but he preferred to be self-sufficient so as not to compromise his integrity (1 Corinthians 9:1–18). In Thessalonica, likewise, Paul and his colleagues toiled night and day, so that 'we might not burden any of you' while proclaiming the gospel of God (1 Thessalonians 2:9; cf. 2 Thessalonians 3:8). He rebukes some who were 'living in idleness, mere busybodies, not doing any work' (2 Thessalonians 3:11).

While the majority of believers appear to have been of humble origins and limited means,[1] a few owned houses large enough to host sizeable groups – like Lydia, the businesswoman who dealt in purple cloth (Acts 16:14–15, 40). She came from Thyatira, which specialized in extracting dye from the madder plant, but was trading in Philippi when she heard and responded to Paul's message. Paul promptly gets into trouble because he delivers a slave girl from 'a spirit of divination'. Her owners are furious because she had 'brought her owners a great deal of money by fortune-telling' (Acts 16:16) and they now see their hope of making money evaporate (16:19).

Paul's activities have a similarly threatening effect on economic interests in Ephesus. Demetrius, a silversmith who made shrines of Artemis, and 'brought no little business to the artisans', sparks a riot when he complains that Paul is persuading people to stop buying silver idols, on the grounds that 'gods made with hands are not gods' (Acts 19:23–28). We see signs of Christian faith subverting the economic order. Industries that exploit people or prey on human weakness or foolishness are threatened, not necessarily by a direct attack on their practices, but by a faithful proclamation of the Gospel – when people become wise to its financial consequences.

In this chapter I shall describe a few influential examples of Christianity's impact on trade during the last 2,000 years.[2]

The active life and the contemplative life: Mary and Martha

First, we must acknowledge that Christian faith can itself be subverted or infiltrated by unhelpful attitudes from the dominant culture. Such was the case in the early church. Greek and Roman thought associated physical work with slaves and artisans, enabling the elite to concentrate on exercising their minds in art, philosophy and politics. Cicero saw the toil of a hired worker and the trade of a small retailer as equally sordid.[3] Eusebius of Caesarea, the early church's leading historian, gave this distinction a religious gloss when he claimed that Christ gave two ways of life to his Church:

> The one is above nature, and beyond common human living: it admits not marriage, child-bearing, property nor the possession of wealth, but, wholly and permanently separate from the common customary life of mankind, devotes itself to service of God alone . . . Such then is the perfect form of the Christian life. And the other, more humble, more human, permits man to join in mere nuptials, and to produce children . . . it allows them to have minds for farming, for trade, and the other more secular interests as well as religion . . . a kind of secondary grade of piety is attributed to them.[4]

Augustine made a similar distinction between the 'active life' and the 'contemplative life'. While both kinds of life were good, and Augustine had words of praise for farmers, craftsmen and merchants, the contemplative life was superior. 'The one life is loved, the other endured.' At times it is necessary to follow the active life, and charity may even oblige it; but 'if no one lays this burden upon us we should give ourselves up to leisure, to the perception and contemplation of truth'.[5]

In making this distinction, Augustine drew on the Gospel story of Mary and Martha (Luke 10:38–42).[6] Martha was distracted by the task of serving Jesus and his disciples, while Mary sat at Jesus' feet and listened to him. When Martha complains that 'my sister has left me to do all the work by myself', Jesus replies: 'Mary has chosen the better part.' Clearly, Christians cannot dispute that it is of primary importance to heed the words of Jesus.

But does this make a life of contemplation superior? Much of Jesus' teaching commends acts of practical service, notably the parables of the good Samaritan and the sheep and the goats. Mary could well have been inspired by listening to Jesus to be of greater use around the house. Martha was so preoccupied that she was in danger of not listening to Jesus at all.

Bill and Irene Manley are an American couple who run a fair trade company called Mary and Martha Mongolia. Bill used to be an oil engineer, Irene a pharmacist. Experiencing a call to mission, they studied for two years at Bible college and felt God guiding them to use their business experience to start a social enterprise in a remote country. The name 'Mary and Martha' reflects their motivation – both love of God and love of neighbour. The company is based in Ulaanbaatar (Ulan Bator), Mongolia's capital, and makes bags, slippers, shawls, stoles and ties, using yarn from camels and yaks. They aim to ensure that their artisans earn one and a half times the minimum national wage.[7]

St Benedict and the monastic orders
The church's exaltation of contemplation led it to prize the monastic life as the highest form of Christian vocation. Monks and nuns felt called to separate themselves from the everyday world of human activities and relationships. What

better way to spend one's time than in contemplative prayer, absorbed in the vision of God, lost in wonder, love and praise? This view appears to leave Christians with little to contribute on the economic front. Surprisingly, monasticism *did* play a positive role in three different ways.

First, *the influence of Benedict's Rule*. The Benedictines, the oldest surviving religious order, date from the foundation of a community at Monte Cassino by St Benedict of Nursia in 529. Benedict wrote a Rule consisting of seventy-five short chapters that has been widely adopted by other orders, each following his advice that different monasteries should arrange matters according to the demands of particular circumstances and cultures. Hallmarks of the Rule are its humanity and balance.

> Benedict's community is founded on prayer, but it is also based on work and community living. A monastery is not a place to which people flee when they cannot face the pressures of work or the demands of living with other people whom they don't much like.[8]

Benedict created a balanced day, in which prayer, work, private reading and time with one another all have their designated place.

The monks lived by the work of their hands: they cultivated and harvested crops for their daily food. Everyone took their turn at routine tasks, though if anyone had particular gifts they were to use them, while needing to avoid the sin of pride.[9] All the monastery's utensils, not just the sacred vessels of the altar, should receive special care. Benedict gives special attention to the Cellarer, the monk with overall responsibility for material and physical goods. He outlines a list of necessary qualities (mature, wise, sober; not a glutton, proud or apt to be irritable) similar to the qualities required of a deacon in 1 Timothy 3. The Cellarer should combine stewardship of things with care for people, as shown in the advice: 'A refusal of a request should be measured and given with due deference towards the person involved.'[10]

Benedict's presentation of the role of Abbot is a profound vision of Christian leadership. It draws on many leadership models found in the Bible: servant, shepherd, teacher, healer/doctor, steward. The Abbot is clearly a man in authority, and should be obeyed; but he also knows how to delegate, listen carefully, show sensitivity to individual needs, respect young and old alike, and set an example in Christ-like behaviour. This model translates well across a range of organizations, including commercial ones. In the UK, the Benedictine abbeys of Douai, Worth and Ampleforth have all run well-attended retreats commending the Rule of St Benedict for busy business leaders.

Second, *the capacity for business innovation.* For several centuries, from about 1100 onwards, monasteries owned large tracts of land in Western Europe, especially France and England. They put this land to productive use. Particularly outstanding were the Cistercians, a reformist group determined to follow the Rule of St Benedict more rigorously. Founded at Citeaux in 1098, they numbered 333 abbeys across Europe by 1152. The Cistercians emphasized the importance of monks doing manual labour, but – recognizing their limits – used lay brothers recruited from the local peasantry to supplement monks' activities and ply useful trades.

The Cistercians were pioneers of medieval technological development. Their formidable list of achievements included:

- grazing of sheep to pioneer the wool and cloth industry, notably in Wales and North Yorkshire

- a well-organized system for selling cattle and horses that they bred
- a vast amount of stone-quarrying for the building of cathedrals and abbeys (not just their own); known as skilled overseers of construction, the Cistercians 'made it a point of honour to recruit the best stone-cutters'[11]
- skilled metallurgy, including the smelting of iron in the Champagne area of France; an early blast furnace at Laskill near Rievaulx Abbey was wastefully destroyed during the Dissolution of the Monasteries
- hydraulic engineering, using large waterwheels for crushing wheat, sieving flour and fulling cloth; a Spanish monastery in Aragon had an elaborate water circulation system for central heating.[12]

The Cistercians combined communal ownership with entre-preneurial flair.

The Scholastic theologians: the just price

Monasticism's third positive contribution to economic life came through *weight of intellectual thought*. Many of the Scholastic theologians or schoolmen who taught economics in the medieval universities of Western Europe were associated with monastic orders. St Thomas Aquinas, Dominican friar and Paris professor, was the most famous.

As Joan O'Donovan says, 'The singular achievement of medieval economic thought was to set economic activity within a dynamic theological understanding of human community as created, fallen, redeemed and sanctified.'[13] This is a community of mutual self-giving, enjoyment and fulfilment in using the earth's abundance, where human beings share in spiritual and material goods. However, they do so under the conditions of fallen nature. The schoolmen's justification of private property was that it curbed the unruly impulses of sinful humanity to appropriate material things in a selfish, violent manner. But private property was still meant to serve the common good. Money, similarly, should function strictly as a medium of exchange; any occupation 'that had the accumulation of monetary wealth as its purpose lay outside the moral boundaries of economic activity'.[14]

The medieval theologians believed in a just price. On the whole, they were happy to accept the market price as just, but they believed in a moral universe that obliged buyers and sellers to act for the common good. They condemned all manipulation of market conditions to yield excessive profits, and every strategy to create and exploit the duress of others. Exploitation included taking advantage of another party's inexperience, ignorance, impulsiveness or simple-mindedness. They compared a poor person obliged to pay an inflated price to sailors in distress forced to ditch merchandise to save themselves and their ship.

The schoolmen listed the items to be taken into account in computing a just price. Franciscan Peter Olivi (1248–98) mentioned labour, expenses, risk, industry and vigil.[15] However, he recognized that exact calculation was impossible, allowing latitude within probable and reasonable limits. Another Franciscan, John Duns Scotus (1265–1308), emphasized the ethical reciprocity of market transactions. Buyers and sellers should make allowance for the fact that they typically have different ideas of what a just price comprises – so a fair outcome usually contains a 'gift' element on both sides.[16] This integrates what the Franciscans saw as the evangelical command to love with the natural law of justice.

Fair trade and just price thinking have much in common. They both advocate good will towards others as a moderating influence on our instinctive acquisitive influences in the marketplace. Yet fair trade supporters haven't drawn on this impressive body of medieval thinking. Even allowing for the schoolmen's analytical shortcomings (and the structural changes in trade that have occurred), they deserve to be better known. Their eclipse can be explained by the fact that, in the following centuries, the restraints they applied to the practice of trade were largely abandoned.

The paradox of riches

Between 1500 and 1750, a major change in the relationship between Christianity and commerce took place. The Protestant Reformation led to a major schism in the Western Church. The monastic orders either went into decline or focused more single-mindedly on a life of prayer, while economic issues ceased to be of significant interest to Roman Catholic theologians. Luther's teaching on vocation provided Protestant Christians with a confident attitude towards work, and Calvin's rethinking on usury heralded a more positive approach to commerce. Both these factors contributed to rapid economic growth in Protestant countries during this period.

For Christians, however, working hard and becoming wealthy are not without problems. The great eighteenth-century Methodist preacher John Wesley saw this with crystal clarity. In a passage cited by Weber, Wesley observed:

> I fear, wherever riches have increased, the essence of religion has decreased in the same proportion. Therefore I do not see how it is possible, in the nature of things, for any revival of true religion to continue long. For religion must necessarily produce both industry and frugality, and these cannot but produce riches. But as riches increase, so will pride, anger, and love of the world in all its branches. How then is it possible that Methodism, that is, a religion of the heart,

though it flourishes now as a green bay tree, should continue
in this state? For the Methodists in every place grow diligent
and frugal; consequently they increase in goods . . .[17]

Wesley was adamant that the solution to this paradox did not
lie in Christians becoming less diligent and frugal. Rather, in
perhaps the most famous sermon ever preached on the use
of money, he exhorted them to *gain all they can* and *save all
they can.*[18]

In saying 'Gain all you can', Wesley makes some careful
qualifications. Means of gain that imperil life or health,
physical or spiritual, our own or our neighbours', are deemed
illegitimate. He rules out occupations that deal in arsenic or
other hurtful minerals, defraud customs, secure loans by
collateral, sell spirits and entice workers from a competitor.
So long as such cautions are observed, Wesley exhorts utter
wholeheartedness:

> Gain all you can by honest industry . . . Lose no time . . . No
> delay!... Put your whole strength to the work. Spare no pains
> . . . You should be continually learning, from the experience
> of others, or from your own experience, reading and
> reflection, to do everything you have to do better today than
> you did yesterday.[19]

Having expounded diligence, Wesley then preaches frugality.
'Save all you can' means 'Expend no part of it merely to
gratify the desire of the flesh, the desire of the eye, or the
pride of life.'[20] He has no time for delicacies, adornments
or concessions to vanity: 'why should you throw away
money upon your children, any more than upon yourself, in
delicate food, in gay or costly apparel, in superfluities of any
kind?'[21]

Wesley's answer to the disturbing trend he identified – for Christians to become rich – lay in his third piece of advice: *give all you can*. Wise and faithful stewardship means:

> First, provide things needful for yourself: food to eat, raiment to put on, whatever nature moderately requires for preserving the body in health and strength. Secondly, provide these for your wife, your children, your servants, or any others who pertain to your household. If when this is done there be an overplus left, then 'do good to them that are of the household of faith.' If there be an overplus still, 'as you have opportunity, do good to all men.'[22]

This is rendering unto God the things that are God's, and Wesley implores his hearers not to stint themselves 'to this or that proportion'.[23] His sermon remains as challenging now as it was then.

Nonconformist employers: Titus Salt

In nineteenth-century Britain a group of industrialists put Wesley's sermon – more or less – into practice. From humble origins they built thriving businesses; their lifestyles were comfortable but far from extravagant; and they gave much of their hard-earned wealth away, either in their lifetime or through generous endowment of trusts. They achieved success in diverse fields: chocolate (George Cadbury); fruit-gums (Joseph Rowntree); biscuits (George Palmer); mustard (Jeremiah James Coleman); medicines (Jesse Boot); soap (William Hesketh Lever); and stockings (Samuel Morley). Ian Bradley, author of a study of these *Enlightened Entrepreneurs*, notes how 'Two belief systems, one political and the other religious, underlay both their commercial enterprise and their philanthropic enlightenment'.[24] The first was

Victorian liberalism, which stood for free trade, self-help, minimal government interference and internationalism. The second was religion of a particular kind – the demanding, rigorous creed of Nonconformity. These employers exemplified the Protestant virtues highlighted by Weber. In Bradley's words 'They were methodical, regular in their habits, relentless in their capacity for hard work and self-improvement, and models of self-discipline and temperance in their personal lifestyles.'[25] Most were teetotallers. They went to bed and rose early, preferring bracing physical exercise to more decadent pleasures.

All this was true of Sir Titus Salt (1803–76), best known for the village he established by the River Aire, Saltaire. As a teenager, Salt was apprenticed to a wool-stapler, where he learned to buy good fleeces at auction, sort out the wool according to the length, softness and fineness of the fibre, and prepare it for spinning into yarn. Already active in a Congregationalist chapel, he joined his father Daniel's firm as a wool buyer before taking it over from him in 1834. Constantly on the lookout for new materials, his breakthrough came when he noticed a pile of 300 dirty-looking bales lying in a Liverpool warehouse. They turned out to be fleeces of the Peruvian alpaca. Impressed by the fibres' straightness and length, he took a sample back to Bradford for experiment. Salt discovered that it produced a high-quality yarn. In 1837 he launched Alpaca Orleans, a fabric made from alpaca and cotton, which became a popular dress material with Victorian ladies. Bradley comments: 'The success of the fabric was assured when Queen Victoria sent Salt the fleeces of the two alpacas she kept in Windsor Park to be made up into cloth.'[26] Salt also introduced the use of mohair, another long-staple combing wool that came from the fleece of the angora goat in Turkey. Through developing the properties of

these two unusual wools, Salt became head of the West
Yorkshire worsted industry.

Mid-nineteenth-century Bradford grew rapidly from a
population of 43,000 to 103,000 between 1831 and 1851. It
was filthy, unhygienic and appalling for children: average
life expectancy was then eighteen years. Over 200 mill
chimneys emitted sulphurous fumes. Salt fitted special
smoke burners to the chimney stacks to reduce pollution
on his five mills. He gave Bradford a sixty-one-acre park so
that people could enjoy some relatively fresh air. Then in
1850 he took the radical step of relocating his company from
the city to a new green-field site three miles north-west of
Bradford.

There Salt erected a new mill, 'the world's first totally
integrated woollen textile factory in which all the processes
from sorting the raw, greasy fleeces to dispatching the dyed
and finished cloth were brought together under one roof'.[27]
It stood six storeys high, with large plate-glass windows
and flues making the building light and airy. Then Salt con-
structed a village of 850 dwellings in twenty-two streets to
accommodate all his 4,500 employees. The houses varied in
size according to the status of the occupants, but they were
all distinct improvements on the cramped and squalid conditions of Bradford. A Congregationalist church, public
baths, school, hospital, library and institute followed, but
no pub: a notice at the entrance to Saltaire said, 'Abandon
beer all ye who enter here.' Salt had witnessed the evils of
over-drinking and was a strict teetotaller. He was an
unashamed paternalist, banning smoking, gambling and
swearing in the village park, but his workers' health benefited
from his concern for their welfare, just as their incomes
did from the company's success. 120,000 people turned out
to pay their tributes when he died.

Enlightened employers were in the minority. Where working conditions were harsh, oppressive and showed no signs of improving, employees had no option but to defend their own interests. Christian socialists were active in the early trade unions, organized in the late nineteenth century to balance the powers of employers and to secure adequate wages and working conditions for their members. Keir Hardie, who led a strike of mineworkers in southern Scotland when owners reduced their wages, learned the art of public speaking as an evangelical preacher; he went on to become the first Independent Labour MP. The claim is often made that 'the Labour Party owed more to Methodism than to Marx',[28] though other Christian churches, especially Roman Catholicism – strong among Irish workers – could claim a significant influence. The political organization of mass labour certainly contributed to a whole raft of reforming UK legislation: the redistribution of wealth through personal and corporate taxation, unemployment benefit, health insurance, and monopoly and competition acts restraining the power of individual companies.[29]

The Eucharist: ordinary made extraordinary

Along with these positive examples from the past, this book contains many examples of contemporary Christians who are making fruitful links between their faith and their work. What unites them is an attitude of dedicating their whole lives, of presenting to God their everyday endeavours in faith that he can do something remarkable with them.

This is memorably expressed in a great hymn written by Victorian Frances Havergal. It begins 'Take my life and let it be / Consecrated Lord to thee' and proceeds to ask that God will make something beautiful of our hands, feet, voice, will, heart, love and very self. It includes the verse:

Take my silver and my gold,
Not a mite would I withhold.
Take my intellect, and use
Every part as Thou shalt choose.

This notion of God taking something ordinary that we offer and doing something extraordinary with it is found at the very heart of the Church's worship, the Eucharist. As American theologian David Jensen writes:

> The central items at the Lord's Table are not wheat and grapes, the raw stuff God gives us, but bread and wine, the products of human labor. Countless hours – indeed, years – of work go into the bread that appears at the Lord's Table each Sunday; tilling soil at the beginning of planting season, sowing seed preserved from last year, watering nascent plants, weeding seedlings, praying for sufficient sun and rain, harvesting grain when it is ripe and golden, threshing wheat from chaff, grinding wheat into flour, mixing flour into dough, stirring in yeast, baking the loaf, bringing bread to market, to say nothing of the hours of planning, research, and transportation involved in each of these steps. The wine, likewise, is the product of endless hours of cultivation, trimming, pressing, fermentation, bottling, and marketing. Vineyards, moreover, do not produce an immediate yield, but require years of labor before even the first fruits appear. These holy things of bread and wine are the products of human hands applied to the bounty God has given; they are there because we work. Without human labor, there is no Eucharist.[30]

This dimension is found in a preface to the Eucharistic prayer used by several churches, and based on Jewish table blessings at the Passover feast:

Blessed are you, Lord God of all creation: through your goodness we have this bread to set before you, which earth has given, and human hands have made. It will become for us the bread of life.
Blessed be God for ever.
Blessed are you, Lord God of all creation: through your goodness we have this wine to set before you, fruit of the vine and work of human hands. It will become for us the cup of salvation.
Blessed be God for ever.

The prayer blesses God, acknowledges his goodness, and looks forward to what the bread and wine will *become*. God provides the soil and seeds; he sends the sun and rain. Human beings are dependent on God, but they are not helpless, ineffectual creatures. As Jensen makes clear, researchers, gardeners, farmers, producers, bakers, bottlers and lorry drivers (among others) all make possible the celebration of the Eucharist.

How wonderful that Jesus chose these two elements as ingredients in this special meal! Bread is a staple food, consumed more regularly by more people worldwide than any other. It *strengthens* the human heart (Psalm 104:15). Jesus is the Bread of Life and whoever comes to him will never be hungry (John 6:35). Wine is a festive drink, convivial, life-enhancing and dangerous if you consume too much. It *gladdens* the human heart (Psalm 104:15). Jesus is the True Vine and his father is the gardener (John 15:1).

The beauty of the Eucharist is that God takes these ordinary products and does something extraordinary with them. As we share the elements, offer ourselves in love and service, remember Jesus' death on the cross, celebrate his coming again, and feed on the bread and the wine, God fulfils our hopes. 'Send your Spirit on us now, that by these gifts we may feed on Christ with opened eyes and hearts on fire.'[31] We are spiritually nourished by Christ, fed and equipped through a God-given means of grace.

The Eucharist is unique, but might not our working lives be transformed if we carried over that attitude of worship from Sunday to Monday? What is to stop us presenting all the objects that we produce, all the services that we offer, and asking for God's blessing on them? God can infuse the ordinary with the extraordinary in the marketplace just as he does in the church building. Jensen gives the seemingly prosaic example of an accountant who 'carefully tabulates expense sheets and keeps budgets so that a shipping company can transport wheat from one end of the Pacific to another'.[32] In knowing that God animates and sustains him in his work, and employing his mathematical gift, he serves others and gives thanks to God.

The Anglican communion service ends with these memorable words: through Christ 'we offer our souls and bodies to be a living sacrifice. Send us out in the power of your Spirit, to live and work to your praise and glory'.[33] The logic of that prayer is the transformation of business. It's a prayer whose outworking we see in the best examples of Christian business practice in past history, from medieval monastic orders to nineteenth-century Nonconformist entrepreneurs.

9. HOPE FOR THE FUTURE: SIGNS OF THE KINGDOM

It may be that you wonder whether a major investment of energy in improving the global economy is really worthwhile. Aren't there clear warnings in Scripture against pinning too many of our hopes and aspirations on earthly – as opposed to heavenly – realities? Hebrews 11 contains poignant remarks about Christian hope. It says the Old Testament heroes of faith saw themselves as 'strangers and foreigners on the earth', and with their forward-looking mentality desired 'a better country, a heavenly one' (Hebrews 11:13–16). An old hymn picks up this theme: 'This earth is not my home, I'm just a-passing through.' If we are strangers and exiles, if our true home or as Paul says our *citizenship* is in heaven (Philippians 3:20), does business actually warrant the careful attention that I am advocating? There is indeed a genuine danger that we could be lured away by preoccupations and pressures which lead us to worship false lords and serve worldly masters, not the God and Father of our Lord Jesus Christ.

Some Christians emphasize the fleeting, transitory nature of the present world. They see the earth as bound for destruction and the after-life as a disembodied sort of existence; their belief is not so much in the resurrection of the body as the immortality of the soul. Heaven is conceived in purely spiritual terms, and our task on earth is to rescue as many people as possible for eternity: hence the frequent talk of 'a hunger for souls'. Evangelism provides an escape route from earth, securing a place in heaven.[1] Christians should not delude themselves that they can build heaven on earth. There is a radical discontinuity between the ages: God is going to destroy the present world completely. Indeed, he may be about to do so very soon; various signs show we are living in the end times.

US-based Croatian theologian Miroslav Volf calls this model *Annihilatio Mundi* (Annihilation of the World) and sums up its implications for work like this:

> If the world will be annihilated and a new one created *ex nihilo*, then mundane work has only earthly significance for the well-being of the worker, the workers' community, and posterity – until the day when 'the heavens will pass away with a loud noise, and the elements will be dissolved with fire' (2 Peter 3:10). Since the results of the cumulative work of humankind throughout history will become naught in the final apocalyptic catastrophe, human work is devoid of direct ultimate significance.[2]

This way of thinking raises two important issues that need addressing: the nature of our future hope and the quality of Christian witness.

Annihilation or transformation?

There is *some* biblical ground for the annihilationist model. On occasion the New Testament talks the language of radical discontinuity. Paul says 'we know that if the earthly tent we live in is destroyed, we have a building from God, a house not made with hands, eternal in the heavens'. He longs to be 'away from the body' and 'at home with the Lord' (2 Corinthians 5:1, 7). 1 Corinthians 15 contrasts the first man who 'was from the earth, a man of dust' with the second man who is 'from heaven', and says 'flesh and blood cannot inherit the kingdom of God' (15:47, 50). 2 Peter 3, quoted above by Volf, is perhaps the strongest assertion about the destruction of the earth.

But even in these three passages, the discontinuity is far from total. 2 Corinthians 5 goes on to describe a 'further clothing' of our earthly tent, so that 'what is mortal may be swallowed up in life' (5:4). 1 Corinthians 15 doesn't ultimately contrast a physical existence with a spiritual existence, more a physical body with a spiritual body (15:44) – though Tom Wright suggests 'spirit-animated' body might be a better translation. Yes, our bodies will be changed, but it will be a case of the perishable body putting on imperishability, and the mortal body putting on immortality (15:54).

Even 2 Peter 3 is not as clear-cut as it initially appears. The phrase in verse 10 often translated 'the earth and everything that is done on it will be burnt up' could refer either to a fire that *destroys* or to a fire which *refines*. The word translated 'burnt up' is itself ambiguous; it could mean 'disclosed' or 'laid bare' – that is, the true nature of the earth will be revealed. But in any case, 2 Peter 3:10 is not the climax of the writer's eschatological vision. His ultimate hope is expressed in verse 13: 'in accordance with God's promise, we wait for new heavens and a new earth, where righteousness is at home.'

It is the biblical passages about a new heaven and a new earth which are fundamental for Christians who take a different view, what Volf calls *Transformatio Mundi* (Transformation of the World). This emphasizes continuity more than discontinuity. Volf comments:

> The picture changes radically with the assumption that the world will not end in apocalyptic destruction but in eschatological transformation. Then the results of the cumulative work of human beings have intrinsic value and gain ultimate significance, for they are related to the eschatological new creation, not only indirectly through the faith and service they enable or sanctification they further,

but also directly: the noble products of human ingenuity, 'whatever is beautiful, true and good in human cultures', will be cleansed from impurity, perfected, and transfigured to become a part of God's new creation. They will form the 'building materials' from which (after they have transfigured) the 'glorified world' will be made.[3]

The phrase 'new heaven and a new earth' is first found in the latter part of the prophet Isaiah (65:17; 66:22). The language is poetic and doubtless symbolic, but there is no mistaking its earthiness. Jerusalem is seen as the focus of a transformed existence. Isaiah 65: 21–22 contains this delightful picture:

> They shall build houses and inhabit them;
> they shall plant vineyards and eat their fruit.
> They shall not build and another inhabit;
> They shall not plant and another eat;
> For like the days of a tree shall the days of my people be,
> And my chosen shall long enjoy the work of their hands.
> They shall not labour in vain, or bear children for calamity . . .

In short, no more frustration, alienation and exploitation! No more expropriation of people's property; no more hostile takeovers. People will be able to enjoy their work, because it will last. They will be able to live in security. This vision of a Golden Age may not be realized this side of eternity, but note that a transformation of work is fundamental to it.

The hope of a future world where everything is in perfect harmony reappears at the Bible's end, in Revelation 21. Again, the language is of a new heaven and a new earth, though the seer also speaks of 'a holy city, the new Jerusalem, coming down out of heaven from God prepared as bride adorned for her husband'. God will dwell among his people, and will wipe every tear from their eyes; 'death will be no more' (Revelation 21:3–4; cf. 7:17). There is no longer any need for a temple, a special holy place, because the city's 'temple is the Lord God Almighty and the Lamb' (21:22). The demarcation between sacred and secular will have broken down forever.

There are other New Testament passages that emphasize the element of continuity: transformation rather than replacement of the existing order. In Matthew 19:28, responding to a question from Peter, Jesus speaks of 'the renewal of all things, when the Son of Man is seated on the throne of glory . . . ' The word 'renewal' is *palingenesis* – literally 'genesis again'. Peter may have taken these words to heart, because in his Acts 3 speech he says that Jesus 'must remain in heaven until the time of universal restoration that God announced long ago through his holy prophets' (Acts 3:21). The *time of universal restoration* and *the renewal of all things* are surely the same.

All things

The phrase 'all things' also appears in Paul's great passage on the person and work of Christ, Colossians 1:15–20. Here Paul portrays Jesus as both lord of the universe and head of the Church. He is the 'image of the invisible God, the firstborn of all creation' (1:15), as well as 'firstborn from the dead' (1:18). Fascinatingly, the word 'things' appears six times and 'everything' once:

- In Christ all things in heaven and on earth were created (1:16).
- These things were created through him and for him (1:17).
- Christ is before all things, and in him all things hold together (1:17).

- He will come to have first place in everything (1:18).
- Through Christ God was pleased to reconcile to himself all things (1:20).

Human beings are infinitely precious in God's sight, and, understandably, when we consider God's purposes in salvation, we think principally of people being reconciled to him. But this passage says that God's saving purposes entail *things* as well. What are these things?

Paul says they are 'things visible and invisible, whether thrones or dominions or rulers or powers' (Colossians 1:16). These seem to be the rulers and authorities which he describes as the 'cosmic powers of this present darkness' and 'the spiritual forces of evil in the heavenly places' in Ephesians 6:12. But his scope here runs wider than that. They are things *visible* as well as invisible, both *on earth* and in heaven. The phrase appears to include all that wield authority. Caesar and the Roman Empire probably loomed large in Paul's mind. Today, along with countries that occupy or aspire to 'super-power' status, we might mention the media, the Internet, the advertising industry or even the global market economy. These are all forces that wield formidable power, in ways seen and unseen. Although they can be used for good, they often seem to be in the grip of evil: the sinister heavenly forces subvert earthly realities. Colossians 1 reassures us that though these things are powerful, they don't possess ultimate power. Created in and by Christ, they are reconciled through 'the blood of his cross' (1:20). The great global forces find their true meaning and fulfilment when subject to Jesus Christ.

The first step towards this may occur when those with mighty power are forced to apologize for abusing it – as when Rupert Murdoch and News International printed full-page advertisements saying 'We're sorry' for serious wrongdoing in all the UK's national newspapers.[4]

'Things' also means the world of material, manufactured things that business produces. Along with products of excellent quality, there are those that are damaged and rejected. Things go wrong in industrial processes. We saw in chapter 4 how events like earthquakes, which damage wine vats and destroy houses as well as killing people, contribute to a creation that is 'in bondage to decay' and 'groaning in labour pains' (Romans 8:21–22). The Christian hope, however, is that the creation will be liberated from this, obtaining the 'freedom of the glory of the children of God': another clear statement that salvation embraces not just us but the world we inhabit. We may be pleasantly surprised to discover in the transformed creation some of our products, purged of their defects and made fully fit for purpose.[5]

Intriguingly, Revelation 21 speaks of people bringing into the heavenly city 'the glory and honour of the nations' (21:24–26). Commentator Michael Wilcock takes this to mean: 'all that is truly good and beautiful will reappear there, purified and enhanced in the perfect setting its Master intended for it; nothing of real value is lost.'[6] What people do in this life is swept up into God's eternal purposes – a point well made, as I commented earlier, by Tom Wright.[7] The products of business endeavour are as likely to feature in this glorious new creation as those of other human activities.

As we have seen, Revelation 21 and the later chapters of Isaiah share common images and concepts. Revelation 21:24–26 is close to Isaiah 60:11: 'Your gates shall always be open; day and night they shall not be shut, so that nations shall bring you their wealth, with their kings led in procession.' The prophet pictures the holy city, a transformed Jerusalem, as a centre of commerce, a place that receives vessels, goods and animals that are beasts of burden.

Richard Mouw, author of a fascinating study of Isaiah 60, asks: why are the ships of Tarshish (60:9) and the cedars of Lebanon (60:13) so prominent in this vision? He notes how in Isaiah 2 they are symbols of cultural arrogance. The Lord of hosts 'has a day against all that is proud and lofty' and both are listed among the items that represent the 'haughtiness of peoples' (Isaiah 2:12–17). The beautifully crafted ships of Tarshish 'were possessions that engendered pride in their owners and crews, instruments of pagan commercial power'.[8] But in the later vision they no longer flaunt alien power; the ships bring silver and gold into the city (60:9). Similarly, 'the glory of Lebanon' is made to beautify God's sanctuary (60:14). Objects cleansed of their idolatrous functions become fitting instruments of service for God and his people. The kings of the nations (who are also mentioned in Revelation 21:24) are made to eat humble pie. As rulers, they both are particularly prone to the corruption of power and symbolize the faults of a national culture. God's judgment entails bending them to a servant role (Isaiah 60:10). The picture is again transformative rather than destructive.

Mouw makes a telling application of this chapter to the present day:

> God will stand in judgment of all idolatrous and prideful attachments to military, technological, commercial, and cultural might. He will destroy all of those rebellious projects that glorify oppression, exploitation, and the accumulation of possessions. It is in such projects that we can discern our own ships of Tarshish and cedars from Lebanon . . . But the 'stuff' of human cultural rebellion will nonetheless be gathered into the Holy City. God still owns the 'filling'. The earth – including

the American military and French art and Chinese medicine and Nigerian agriculture – belongs to the Lord. And he will reclaim all of these things, harnessing them for service in the City.[9]

Effective Christian witness

What, then, becomes of our concern for rescuing the lost? Is this rendered irrelevant by a future hope that speaks of God transforming his creation? Not so. Rather, we must emphasize the latter in order to recover a proper biblical balance.

Clearly, God's love for the individual sinner is crucial to the gospel message. Jesus meets us one-to-one, just as he did with Zacchaeus and the Samaritan woman during his days on earth. Our response to him may separate us from members of our own family (Matthew 10:34–39). Everyone must stand before the judgment seat of God and give personal account to him (Romans 14:10–12; cf. 2 Corinthians 5:10). Individual names are written in the Lamb's book of life (Revelation 13:8, 21:27). Witness to others, including friends and colleagues at work, will often involve engaging with them about deeply personal matters – perhaps issues of anguish, anger, hurt and guilt that have surfaced through their most intimate relationships.

But 'no man is an island'.[10] We all live and work in particular contexts and cultures. The prophetic strands of the Bible talk about social groups and nations coming under God's judgment and experiencing his redemption. Jesus, the lamb who was slain, is also the lamp who lights up the transformed city. The leaves of the tree of life 'are for the healing of the nations' (Revelation 22:2). Our witness to others includes having something to say about the broader, cultural and organizational issues that occupy those around us. If we are true to the overall thrust of the Bible, this message has positive as well as negative content: words of hope as well as words of judgment. Even words of judgment can be positive if they elicit a response of faith, contrition and changed ways.

People I know with long experience of business are convinced that Christian witness is far more credible when you can show that your faith has something to say about the issues with which your company is grappling. Jim Wright, former Human Resources Director for Research & Development at SmithKline Beecham (now GlaxoSmithKline) argued this at a Ridley conference. He said it is important to recognize that many of the issues people face at work are to do with fundamental meaning. He highlighted:

- organizational purpose – is this simply increasing shareholder value, providing goods and services of value to the customer, or meeting the needs of stakeholders more widely?
- organizational values – what are they, is the company serious about implementing them, and how can staff support and challenge each other in this area more constructively?
- understanding of human nature – what motivates people at work, do we assume the worst or appeal to the best in them, and can we model processes that demonstrate trust, delegate responsibility and embody mutual accountability?
- relationships – is care given to the quality of these, what investment is put into developing people, and how can forgiveness and reconciliation be practised?
- busyness – what can be done to counter-act the 'hurry culture' that causes stress and anxiety, and damages the quality of relationships?

- work-life balance – what is an appropriate balance, or is this a misguided concept that needs replacing by an integration of different spheres of life?

Faith provides a helpful perspective on all these issues. Christians should be able to 'speak into' corporate discussions, making a distinctive contribution and explaining the reasons for their thinking as appropriate.

Jim observed that it might appear ridiculous to talk about the value of love in a business setting – but he relayed an experience that suggests otherwise:

> I was mediating in a conflict between two senior vice-presidents, who were having what they thought was a private turf war, but the people in their organisations were aware that it was going on and were taking their cues from their leaders. I said to one, 'You have been appointed to work together as colleagues to lead the organisation. How would you act differently if you really loved your colleague?' The question stopped him in his tracks and led the discussion in a totally different direction. To cut a long story short, I had a lump in my throat when they stood on the platform together at a joint gathering of their staff, confessed their feuding, said that it was an end, and embraced each other. That shows the power of the name of love.[11]

Note how Jim's unexpected and courageous intervention provided the crucial breakthrough in a messy corporate situation.

Jim describes this approach as *reclaiming business for the kingdom of God*. Business rightly belongs under God's rule, but largely acts independently of him. As the people of God, Christians need to act with the authority God provides to engage in debate about basic organizational principles. Because ignoring of these principles leads to personal dissatisfaction and organizational dysfunction, there is a real chance of being heard. Jim is hopeful that we can reclaim lost ground in terms of the kingdom of God impacting upon organizational life.[12]

Signs of the kingdom

Is this way of thinking about the kingdom justified? I believe so. Whether we embrace it depends very much on the nature of our future hope. According to Moltmann, 'Christianity is eschatology, is hope . . . revolutionizing and transforming the present'[13] The hope for a better world we have as Christians ought to excite and motivate us so much – we should embrace it so eagerly – that we allow it to change our present. Although we may not realise it, this is essentially what we ask every time we pray the Lord's Prayer. Such hope is intrinsically connected to Jesus' teaching about the kingdom of God.

What, after all, does it mean to request 'Your kingdom come'? The very next phrase supplies the answer: that God's will be done on earth, as perfectly as it is in heaven – the place where God's rule is undisputed. In James Jones' memorable words, we pray for 'the earthing of heaven',[14] though 'the heavening of earth' would be equally appropriate. God's will was also perfectly executed by Jesus himself during his time on earth. The kingdom has dawned in Jesus, but it is incomplete, and it will only arrive fully with his second coming. Nevertheless, the ministry of Jesus in word and deed – the example of complete dedication to his Father's will – has given us a picture of what that kingdom is like. We look and work for signs of the kingdom, in our organizations as in other areas of life.

If we are sincere in making the request that God's kingdom should come, then we open ourselves up to the possibility that it will indeed be granted, that we may actually be agents of doing God's will. By simple acts of obedient discipleship, we play a part in bringing the present world more into conformity with that glorious future age of which the biblical passages speak. Situations, not just individuals, can be changed for the better.

In the world that we know we may only get occasional glimpses of this, but there *are* moments worth savouring. Just as there are episodes of depressing futility in life and frustration at work, so there can also be moments of exciting transformation. Signs of the kingdom might include:

- the unravelling of manipulative accounting practice, so that confusion and cover-up are stripped away, and the true state of financial affairs is clearly revealed. Although the situation looks bleak, progress can be made now that people know where they stand
- a breakthrough in negotiating a contract, when over a meal seller and buyer succeed not just in agreeing a price, but discover unexpected synergies through working in partnership, as well as getting into a deep conversation about meaning and purpose in life
- the restoration of a marriage that had been on the rocks due to a husband spending an inordinate amount of time on foreign business trips which were a source of sexual temptation. Having taken advice from a Christian friend, he seeks and obtains a home-based job from his firm and forgiveness from his wife.

In previous chapters I have given several instances of organizations where kingdom 'moments' are a regular occurrence:

T. S. Wong, modelling good working practice in China; Flowering Desert, the place of refuge for women sewing beautiful products in Tamil Nadu; Lautaro Wines, showing solidarity for those hit hardest by natural disaster in the Curico Valley . . . to name but a few. Here is another example, a genuine sign of hope.

Broetje Orchards is a 5,000–acre apple orchard in south-east Washington state. The company packs over 5 million boxes of apples a year and sells them to America's leading retailers under the brand-name First Fruits of Washington – inspired by the biblical festival in Deuteronomy 26 where people offered the first and best of their harvests to God. Operating in a sector which employs many seasonal workers with all the family disruption that causes, owners Ralph and Cheryl Broetje have deliberately created more full-time employment through establishing a community alongside the business. Among other facilities they have built 100 two-, three- and four-bedroom homes, a Christian school, a day-centre and a ranch for troubled youths. The company donates over 60% of its after-tax profits to local, domestic and international projects. Its motto is 'A quality fruit company committed to "bearing fruit that will last"' (John 15:16). Broetje Orchards is into developing people as well as selling excellent apples.[15]

Work and worship

My conviction is that Christian hope for the future should cause us to strive for transformation in the present world, not deter us. This is because 'Through the Spirit, God is already working in history, using human actions to create provisional states of affairs that anticipate the new creation in a real way'.[16] It is right to be delighted when substantial progress is made in the direction of any one of them. But that is nothing to the excitement there will be when God brings his great work to completion!

That completion is dominated by the theme of *worship*. The New Testament contains some memorable pictures of Father and Son receiving the worship they deserve – a worship all too often denied to them on earth. Paul speaks of every knee bending at the name of Jesus, and every tongue confessing that Jesus Christ is Lord. In Revelation 5 the myriad worshippers of heaven sing with full voice the great hymn 'Worthy is the Lamb!' The impression we get of the new heaven and the new earth is that most of our creative energies will go into worshipping God: 'the throne of God and of the Lamb' will be there, and 'his servants will worship him' (Revelation 22:3).

There is a close etymological link between the words 'worship' and 'work'; the Hebrew word *avodah* actually means both. Liturgy, likewise, means 'work of the people'. Worship, carried out well, contains an undeniable element of work. The worship we will offer to God in a renewed creation will be work translated and transformed into another dimension. It will engage the energies and talents of all God's faithful people, whatever the type of work they have done on earth.

10. FAITH, HOPE AND LOVE: AN ALTERNATIVE VISION FOR BUSINESS

In a speech delivered to the Senate House at Cambridge University in 1857, the Scottish missionary-doctor David Livingstone said 'those two pioneers of civilisation – Christianity and commerce – should ever be inseparable.'[1] He was excited both by the prospects of bringing the gospel to the peoples of central Africa, notably Zambia, and by the rich agricultural produce of their fertile lands. Although his motives might sound suspiciously mixed, Livingstone genuinely believed that trade – other than the obnoxious slave trade – would benefit Africans as well as Europeans.

In this book I have sought to establish a positive connection between Christianity and commerce. The Christian faith – rightly understood – can be a power for good in the global economy. We have seen examples of countries and companies, cultures and individuals, where this is demonstrably the case. But do these carefully selected examples give us a true picture? There are two reasons to believe they do.

First, a worldwide survey conducted by the US National Bureau of Economic Research on Religion and Economic Attitudes found that, on average, religious beliefs are associated with 'good' economic attitudes.[2] 'Good' was defined as conducive to higher *per capita* income and growth. Religious people tend to trust each other, their government and the legal system more than average, to be less willing to break the law, and more likely to believe that markets' outcomes will be fair.[3] Overall Christianity is more positively associated with attitudes conducive to economic growth than other faiths.

Second, my argument is not a crudely simplistic 'Christianity is better than the rest'. Some forms of Christianity are emphatically *not* a power for good. Their distorted or one-sided theology (usually emphasizing certain strands of biblical teaching to the neglect of others) means that that they either embrace the prevailing economic system too uncritically, or find nothing good to say about it at all.

In some cultures, Christianity is seen as predominantly a private matter and makes little impact on standards of public behaviour. There are countries where high levels of church attendance co-exist with endemic institutional corruption, highly materialistic mindsets, huge disparities between rich and poor, and a ruthlessly competitive, winner-takes-all form of capitalism. The relationship between Christianity and culture is two-way. Jesus uses the image of leaven both positively (e.g. Matthew 13:33) and negatively (e.g. Matthew 16:6). Penetration takes place in both directions, for good and evil.

In addition, there are certainly examples of other cultures and religions proving a power for good in the global economy. Christianity has a shared heritage with Judaism, and Jews have often been at the forefront of economic activity and innovation. Confucianism emphasizes the importance of loyalty, meritocracy and study of knowledge. The Confucian background is probably a significant factor in recent economic growth in Korea and China. In the chapter on Korea in his magisterial study *Trust*, Francis Fukuyama suggests that 'both Protestant and Confucian cultures promote similar kinds of economic and entrepreneurial values'.[4]

With these careful qualifications, I stand by my basic argument. To understand Christian faith rightly, one needs a thorough, in-depth, well-integrated engagement with the Bible, from Genesis to Revelation. Too many theologies of work fizzle out after a study of Genesis 1–3, or apply Old

Testament law in too wooden a fashion. Alongside the Hebrew Scriptures, we must do full justice to the life, death and resurrection of Jesus. That is why we have looked at each important stage in his ministry. I have presented the biblical story as a drama in seven parts, each with ramifications for business.

The exciting news is that we are active participants in the drama: the ramifications are consequences that it is our responsibility to work out. Living in act six, looking back to acts one to five and forward to act seven, we can play a small but real part by entering responsibly into the drama and improvising appropriately.[5]

Taken overall, this is a profoundly hopeful story. It certainly includes scenes of deep disappointment, devastating failure, heart-breaking tragedy and severe warning. But the central thrust is positive. God has not given up on his world and he has a glorious future in store for it. He calls, desires and equips his people to play their part in making a difference. In the economic sphere they do this by stimulating enterprise, reducing poverty, promoting integrity, ensuring sustainability and fostering discipleship. Taken together, these activities point in a clear direction: *transformation* of the global economy.

Transformation, a theme which has featured prominently in previous chapters, has become a fashionable word in Christian 'faith and business' circles. It came into popular usage through Richard Niebuhr's book *Christ and Culture*, which presented and critiqued four different typologies for understanding the relationship between Christ and culture (Christ against culture, Christ of culture, Christ above culture, Christ and culture in paradox), but was more positive about a fifth type, Christ the transformer of culture.[6] The *leitmotif* of a recent American book commending a Christian vision for the marketplace is 'transformational service for the common good'.[7] Transformational Business Network and Transforming Business are two notable UK organisations which promote enterprise-based solutions to poverty.[8]

However, it is all too easy to use transformation as a rather woolly, feel-good word, while leaving important questions about the global economy unanswered. Let me clarify where I stand.

Alternative business models

In this book I have deliberately given a considerable proportion of space to types of business that fall outside the mainstream: social enterprise, fair trade, micro-credit, cooperatives and eco-friendly companies. Their emergence is one of the most positive developments in the contemporary global economy. Social enterprise is channelling entrepreneurial flair to help the poor and marginalized. Fair trade is challenging consumers' self-interest in securing better pay and conditions for producers in developing countries. Micro-credit is offering loans designed to help the poor rather than exploit them. Cooperatives are a more democratic form of structuring companies that remove the impersonal shareholder dimension and reduce extreme pay differentials. Eco-friendly companies offer resource-efficient products and services that promise environmental sustainability. Taken together, they do much to promote the five-fold aims I have set out.

None of them is a panacea. There are real questions about their effectiveness, some of which I have sought to address in earlier chapters. None of them escape the dark shadow cast by the fall; all can come into the hands of the dishonest, unscrupulous or plain incompetent. But as I have travelled the world, I have seen impressive examples of each in action.

I believe that together they comprise part of the answer to the world's problems – though not the whole answer.

Social enterprise, fair trade, micro-credit, cooperatives and eco-friendly companies are a series of *alternative business models*. They operate on different assumptions from conventional business. Financial results matter, but they are not the ultimate measurement of success as with the majority of companies. If every company were to operate on an alternative business model, we would indeed have an alternative economic system.

Alternative business models are undoubtedly on the increase. According to UN estimates, cooperatives employ over 100 million people around the world and 800 million are members of cooperatives, touching the lives of as many as 3 billion.[9] These alternatives operate within the global capitalist system. Capitalism's dominant model remains the public limited company, and the most powerful agents in the global economy are multinational PLCs. Nevertheless, capitalism does not prescribe or dictate a single corporate structure. Capitalism is concerned with the increase of capital, but it does not dictate *how* capital is increased. One of its strengths is that it is open to all kinds of business models, companies based on a variety of formats and philosophies – differences that don't prevent them from doing business with each other.

Working for big companies

Furthermore, some conventional companies show plenty of positive qualities. There are good people and socially responsible units operating across the corporate spectrum; alternative business models do not have a monopoly on the virtues of enterprise, integrity and sustainability. Where Corporate Social Responsibility is taken seriously and is more than a sop to public opinion, multinational companies seek to be accountable in all their stakeholder relations. In some areas they succeed better than others; but they deserve credit when they get things right.

Though BP, for instance, may have seriously blotted its copybook with accidents that have happened in the USA, it has taken a commendable lead with its 'zero tolerance' position on bribery, notably in relation to the EITI (Extractive Industries Transparency Initiative). This requires full publication and verification of payments by companies to governments and of governments' revenues from oil, gas and mining.[10] Johnson & Johnson may have had their share of problematic products, but have always acted with exemplary speed in recalling those that endangered the public – most famously in 1982 when they pulled 31 million bottles of Tylenol (paracetamol) capsules off the shelves nationwide after a murderer penetrated a few bottles in Chicago with cyanide, killing seven people. Improved tamper-proof, triple-sealed safety containers were on the shelves ten weeks after the withdrawal. The episode cost Johnson & Johnson more than $100 million, but before long it recovered its market share. The company is guided by the most impressive of mission statements, the J&J Credo, formulated by founder Robert Wood Johnson in 1943, which is clear that 'our first responsibility is to the doctors, nurses and patients, to mothers and father and all others who use our services'.[11]

There is a very important place, then, for Christians working in big companies, winning respect by being effective at their jobs, and keeping corporate standards up to the mark or helping to improve them. Clearly someone in a senior position can do this more easily, but those who occupy junior positions and doubt their capacity to influence corporate affairs may be encouraged by the following story.

It was told by a young woman who shared her experience at a London Institute for Contemporary Christianity event:

> I work for an investment bank where I was recently part of a team involved in a major deal. The Directors in the team decided that they would be economical with the truth in what they communicated to the minority shareholders. I knew this was wrong, but as a junior in the team, didn't feel that I could influence the decision. But after a sleepless weekend I decided to speak out at a teleconference in which all the big hitters in our team, including our external lawyers, were participating. Sick with apprehension, I shared my concerns about the lack of integrity, its damaging effects on the minority shareholders and the potential for damaging the bank if the dishonesty was discovered. My intervention was greeted with a shocked silence, but eventually the directors decided to revise their plans and communicate openly with the minority shareholders.[12]

Not only did that young woman play a vital part in safeguarding her firm's reputation, she also took a step in developing her own character that will help her deal with future challenges to her integrity and courage.

A corporate decision to be honest rather than dishonest may fall far short of the transformation I have in mind. Nevertheless, small victories in preventing wrongdoing are not to be underestimated. Christians are to be salt of the earth (Matthew 5:13). We think of salt as providing additional taste and enhancing flavour, but in the ancient world it was used as a preservative, to stop things from going bad. Christians can be a force for good in the global economy in many different ways, great and small.

Faith, hope and love

The year is 588 BC. The Babylonian army is hammering at the gates of Jerusalem. The prophet Jeremiah is under arrest as a traitor in the court of King Zedekiah because he has predicted the city's downfall as punishment for the nation's unfaithfulness. Hanamel, Jeremiah's cousin, can see the writing on the wall: the only way to escape from poverty is to sell his property. Despite the fact that no-one was more convinced that the Babylonians would take the city than Jeremiah, he does his duty as kinsman-redeemer and accepts Hanamel's request that he buy the field. The transaction is described in graphic detail:

> And I bought the field at Anathoth from my cousin Hanamel, and weighed out the money to him, seventeen shekels of silver. I signed the deed, sealed it, got witnesses, and weighed the money on scales. Then I took the sealed deed of purchase, containing the terms and conditions, and the open copy and I gave the deed of purchase to Baruch son of Neraiah son of Mahseiah, in the presence of my cousin Hanamel . . . I charged Baruch, saying, Thus says the Lord of hosts, the God of Israel: Take these deeds, both this sealed deed of purchase and this open deed, and put them in an earthenware jar, in order that they may last for a long time. For thus says the Lord of hosts, the God of Israel: Houses and fields and vineyards shall again be bought in this land. (Jeremiah 32:9–15)

The purchase of the field at Anathoth is no ordinary business transaction. Jeremiah himself never benefited from it. After the fall of Jerusalem, some Jewish refugees fled to Egypt, taking Jeremiah with them (Jeremiah 43:5–7). As far as we know, he never returned.

Nevertheless, Jeremiah's action was a powerful prophetic gesture. He acted as he did not on his own behalf, but in response to God's command and as an expression of hope for his younger compatriots. He was demonstrating that though the short-term prospect was bleak, *they* had a long-term future. His situation was unusual, his property purchase amidst a national crisis audacious. But the story does illustrate three important lessons.

First, investments can be long-term rather than short-term. National crises pass; economic downturns level out eventually. The property developer who picks up a plot of land dirt-cheap at the bottom of the market may be on to something lucrative if he keeps it long enough. Africa is the world's poorest continent, racked by numerous problems, but there are clear indications that it now offers promising investment opportunities. Hope needs to be allied with *faith*. Such an attitude marks many Western Christians investing in social enterprises in the developing world today.

Second, an investment has a different character if made not principally for oneself, but on behalf of others. Buying the Anathoth field was intended to encourage Jeremiah's youthful contemporaries. His people faced the heartbreak of exile, but it wouldn't last for ever; normal business would one day resume in the Jerusalem area. The transaction bore the marks not just of hope and faith, but of *love*. St Paul juxtaposed these three virtues in 1 Corinthians 13:13: 'And now faith, hope and love abide, these three; and the greatest of these is love.' Yes indeed. Faith and hope are powerful motivators, but they can lose their spark. They need to be kindled by love, that active compassion which reaches out to change the fortunes of people who have odds stacked against them. Long-term investment can express and embody love of neighbour, whether near or far away, and bring hope to a global economy that in many respects is built on selfishness.

Third, business transactions carried out in obedience to God's commands can defy normal commercial criteria. Jeremiah bought the field in response to a 'word of the Lord'. God may still lead his people to perform unlikely transactions today. Clearly one must be careful here. 'Words from the Lord' too easily turn out to be figments of deluded imagination. But if God spoke *then*, he can also speak *now*. What is to stop the Holy Spirit inciting acts of adventure that flout conventional business wisdom but ultimately prove shrewd speculation?

Let us take to heart the famous prayer of Sir Francis Drake:

Disturb us, Lord, to dare more boldly, to venture on wider seas, where storms will show your mastery; where losing sight of land, we shall find the stars. We ask you to push back the horizons of our hopes, and to guide us into the future in strength, courage, hope and love.

BIBLIOGRAPHY

Books

Bernard Adeney, *Strange Virtues: Ethics in a Multicultural World*, IVP, 1995.

Aquinas, *Summa Theologica*, Benziger, 1947.

Augustine, *City of God*, Penguin, 1972.

Beatriz Armedavic, *The Economics of Microfinance*, MIT Press, 2005.

Daryl Balia, *Make Corruption History*, SPCK, 2009.

Robert Banks, *God the Worker: Journeys into the Mind, Heart and Imagination of God*, Judson Press, 1994.

Karl Barth, *Church Dogmatics* III:3, T. & T. Clark, 1976.

Craig Blomberg, *Neither Poverty nor Riches: A Biblical Theology of Possessions*, Apollos, 1999.

Ian Bradley, *Enlightened Entrepreneurs: Business Ethics in Victorian Britain*, Lion Hudson, 2007.

Richard Branson, *Business Stripped Bare: Adventures of a Global Entrepreneur*, Virgin Books, 2008.

John Browne, *Beyond Business: An Inspirational Memoir from a Remarkable Leader*, Phoenix, 2011.

Richard Burridge, *Imitating Jesus: An Inclusive Approach to New Testament Ethics*, Eerdmans, 2007.

Vince Cable, *The Storm: The World Economic Crisis and What It Means*, Atlantic, 2009.

G. B. Caird, *The Gospel of St Luke*, Pelican, 1963.

John Calvin, *Calvin's Ecclesiastical Advice*, Westminster / John Knox Press, 1991.

John Calvin, *Commentaries on the Four Last Books of Moses*, Eerdmans, 1950.

Jim Collins, *How the Mighty Fall And Why Some Companies Never Give In*, Random House, 2009.

Darrell Cosden, *The Heavenly Good of Earthly Work*, Paternoster, 2006.

Marva J. Dawn, *The Sense of the Call: A Sabbath Way of Life for Those Who Serve God, the Church, and the World*, Eerdmans, 2006.

Kit Dollard, Anthony Marett-Crosby and Abbot Timothy Wright, *Doing Business with Benedict*, Continuum, 2002.

Shirley K. Drew, Melanie Mills and Bob Gassway, *Dirty Work: The Social Construction of Taint*, Baylor University Press, 2007.

Tarek El Diwany (ed.), *Islamic Banking and Finance*, 1st Ethical Charitable Trust, 2010.

Ken Eldred, *God is at Work: Transforming People and Nation through Business*, Manna Ventures, 2005.

David Erdal, *Local Heroes: How Loch Fyne Oysters Embraced Employee Ownership*, Random House, 2008.

David Erdal, *Beyond the Corporation: Humanity Working*, Random House, 2011.

Alain Erlande-Brandenburg, *The Cathedral Builders of the Middle Ages*, Thames & Hudson, 1993.

Eusebius, *Demonstration of the Gospel*, SPCK, 1920.

Amintore Fanfani, *Catholicism, Protestantism and Capitalism*, IHS Press, 2003.

Niall Ferguson, *Empire: How Britain Made the Modern World*, Penguin, 2003.

Niall Ferguson, *The Ascent of Money: A Financial History of the World*, Penguin, 2008.

Niall Ferguson, *Civilization: The West and the Rest*, Allen Lane, 2011.

T. E.Fretheim, *Exodus*, John Knox Press, 1991.

Francis Fukuyama, *Trust: The Social Virtues and the Creation of Prosperity*, Penguin, 1995.

Jean Gimpel, *The Medieval Machine: The Industrial Revolution of the Middle Ages*, Rinehart and Winston, 1976.

Richard J. Goossen (ed.), *Entrepreneurial Leaders: Reflections on Faith at Work III*, Trinity Western University, 2007.

Richard J. Goossen (ed.), *Entrepreneurial Leaders: Reflections on Faith at Work IV*, Trinity Western University, 2008.

Timothy Gorringe, *Capital and the Kingdom: Theological Ethics and Economic Order*, SPCK, 1994.

Timothy Gorringe, *Fair Shares: Ethics and the Global Economy*, Thames & Hudson, 1999.

Mark Greene, *The Great Divide*, LICC, 2010.

Stephen Halliday, *The Great Stink of London: Joseph Bazalgette and the Cleansing of the Victorian Metropolis*, The History Press Ltd, 2001.

Charles Hampden-Turner and Fons Trompenaars, *The Seven Cultures of Capitalism*, Little, Brown, 1995.

Peter Heslam, *Transforming Capitalism: Entrepreneurship and the Renewal of Thrift*, Grove Ethics no.156, 2010.

Richard Higginson, *Questions of Business Life*, Authentic Media, 2002.

Richard Higginson and David Clough, *The Ethics of Executive Pay*, Grove Ethics no.159, 2010.

Richard Horsley, *Jesus and the Spiral of Violence: Popular Jewish Resistance in Rural Palestine*, Augsburg Fortress, 1992.

David H. Jensen, *Responsive Labor: A Theology of Work*, Westminster/John Knox Press, 2006.

James Jones, *Jesus and the Earth*, SPCK, 2004.

Norman L. Jones, 'Usury' in H. J. Hillerbrand (ed.), *Oxford Encyclopedia of the Reformation* (Oxford University Press, 1996).

Derek Kidner, *Proverbs*, IVP, 2008.

Harriet Lamb, *Fighting the Banana Wars and Other Fairtrade Battles*, Rider & Co, 2008.

David Landes, *The Wealth and Poverty of Nations: Why are Some So Rich and Some So Poor*, WW Norton, 1998.

Odd Langholm, *Economics in the Medieval Schools: Wealth, Exchange, Value, Money and Usury according to the Paris Theological Tradition*, EJ Brill, 1992.

Odd Langholm, *The Legacy of Scholasticism in Economic Thought*, Cambridge University Press, 1999.

C. S.Lewis, *Miracles*, Fontana, 1960.

Martin Luther, 'On Trade and Usury', *Luther's Works*, Vol. 45, Fortress, 1962.

J. W. Marshall, *Israel and the Book of the Covenant: An Anthropological Approach to Biblical Law*, Atlanta, 1993.

David Martin, *Tongues of Fire: The Explosion of Pentecostalism in Latin America*, Wiley-Blackwell, 1993.

Karl Marx, *Economic and Philosophical Manuscripts*, Progress Publishers, 1959.

Andy Matheson, *In His Image*, Authentic Media, 2009.

Ian L. McHarg, *Design with Nature*, Doubleday, 1969.

Paul Mills, 'Finance' in Michael Schluter and John Ashcroft, *The Jubilee Manifesto: A Framework, Agenda and Strategy for Christian Social Reform*, IVP, 2005.

Sushil Mohan, *Fair Trade Without the Froth*, IEA, 2010.

Jürgen Moltmann, *A Theology of Hope: On the Ground and Implications of a Christian Eschatology*, SCM, 1967.

Jürgen Moltmann, *On Human Dignity: Political Theology and Ethics*, Fortress, 1984.

Jürgen Moltmann, *A Broad Place: An Autobiography*, SCM, 2007.

George Moody-Stuart, *Grand Corruption: How Business Bribes Damage Developing Countries*, WorldView Publishing, 1997.

Richard Mouw, *When the Kings Come Marching In: Isaiah and the New Jerusalem*, Eerdmans, 1983.

H. Richard Niebuhr, *Christ and Culture*, Harper & Row, 1951.

Reinhold Niebuhr, *Man's Nature and his Communities*, Charles Scribner's Sons, 1965.

John T. Noonan, Jr, *Bribes*, Macmillan, 1984.

Michael Northcott, *A Moral Climate: The Ethics of Global Warming*, DLT, 2007.

Michael Novak, *The Spirit of Democratic Capitalism*, Madison Books, 1982.

Chris Patten, *What Next? Surviving the Twenty-First Century*, Allen Lane, 2008.

Robert Peston, *Who Runs Britain? And Who's to Blame for the Economic Mess We're In*, Hodder & Stoughton, 2008.

Eve Poole, *The Church on Capitalism: Theology and the Market*, Palgrave Macmillan, 2010.

Jean Porter, 'Virtue Ethics', in Robin Gill (ed.), *The Cambridge Companion to Christian Ethics*, Cambridge University Press, 2001.

Simon Schama, *The Embarrassment of Riches: An Interpretation of Dutch Culture in the Golden Age*, Random House, 1987.

Joseph Schumpeter, *Capitalism, Socialism and Democracy*, Harper & Row, 1942.

Adam Smith, *The Wealth of Nations*, Penguin, 1999.

Robert Southey, *Life of Wesley* II, Hutchinson, 1900.

William H. Spohn, *Go and Do Likewise: Jesus and Ethics*, Continuum, 2000.

Susan E. Squires, Cynthia J. Smith, Lorna McDougall and William R. Yeack, *Inside Arthur Andersen: Shifting Values, Unexpected Consequences*, FT Press, 2003.

John Stott, *The Cross of Christ*, IVP, 1986.

Gillian Tett, *Fool's Gold: How Unrestrained Greed Corrupted a Dream, Shattered Global Markets and Unleashed a Catastrophe*, Little, Brown, 2009.

Miroslav Volf, *Work in the Spirit: Toward a Theology of Work*, Oxford University Press, 1991.

James Walvin, *The Quakers: Money and Morals*, John Murray, 1997.

William J. Webb, *Slaves, Women and Homosexuals: Exploring the Hermeneutics of Cultural Analysis*, IVP, 2001.

Max Weber, *The Protestant Ethic and the Spirit of Capitalism*, Routledge Classics, 2001.

Samuel Wells, *Improvisation: The Drama of Christian Ethics*, SPCK, 2004.

Michael Wilcock, *I Saw Heaven Opened: The Message of Revelation*, IVP, 1975.

Wilf Wilde, *Crossing the River of Fire: Mark's Gospel and Global Capitalism*, Epworth, 2006.

Richard Wilkinson and Kate Pickett, *The Spirit Level: Why More Equal Societies Almost Always Do Better*, Allen Lane, 2009.

Ben Witherington III, *Jesus and Money*, SPCK, 2010.

Kenman L. Wong & Scott B. Rae, *Business for the Common Good: A Christian Vision for the Marketplace*, IVP Academic, 2011.

Christopher J. H. Wright, *Deuteronomy*, Hendrickson, 1996.

Christopher J. H. Wright, *Old Testament Ethics for the People of God*, IVP, 2004.

Tom Wright, *Surprised by Hope*, SPCK, 2007.

John Howard Yoder, *The Politics of Jesus*, Eerdmans, 1972.

Hwa Yung, *Bribery and Corruption: Biblical Reflections and Case Studies for the Marketplace in Asia*, Graceworks, 2010.

Muhammad Yunus, *Banker to the Poor*, Aurum Press, 1998.

Journal articles, papers and reports

James Allcock, 'Prudence in Business', *FiBQ* 8:2, pp. 14–20.

Allan Bussard, 'Enterprise Solutions to Poverty', *FiBQ* 14:2, pp. 3–6.

Natalie Man Se Chan, 'Making Toys in China', *FiBQ* 13:2, pp. 23–25.

Child Workers in Asia, *Understanding Bonded Child Labour*. 2007.

Sang-Goog Cho, 'Korean Economy: A Model Case of Miraculous Growth?', unpublished paper, 1993.

Egan Report, *Rethinking Construction*, 1998.

Peter Frost and Sandra Robinson, 'The Toxic Handler: Organizational Hero – and Casualty', *Harvard Business Review*, July-August 1999, pp. 97–106.

Brian Griffiths, 'The case for usury: Biblical foundations of a modern credit economy', *FiBQ* 10:2, pp. 23–27.

Luigi Guiso, Paolo Sapienza and Luigi Zingales, *People's Opium? Religion and Economic Attitudes*, NBER Working Paper 9237, October 2002.

Peter Heslam, 'Boss Christians: Entrepreneurs in Asia's Spiritual and Economic Awakening', *FiBQ* 13:3, pp. 31–32.

Peter Heslam, 'Savings on a Passage to India: from Debt to Equity in a Subprime World', *FiBQ* 13:4, pp. 29–30.

Richard Higginson, 'Can Business Be Christian? A report on a Ridley Hall Foundation conference', *FiBQ* 7:3.

John Hughes, 'Work, prayer and leisure in the Christian tradition', *Crucible*, Jan-Mar 2011

Latham Report, *Constructing the Team*, 1994.

David H. Jensen, 'Fed and Hungry at Christ's Table: Daily Work and the Abundance of Eucharist', *FiBQ* 11:1, pp. 3–7.

John Lovatt, 'Jesus in the Workplace: Towards a Better Theology of Work'. *MC*, 1992, Vol. XXXIV, No. 2.

John Lovatt, 'All Things', *FiBQ* 13:2, pp. 3–11.

Mark McAllister, 'An Inconvenient Truth', *FiBQ* 13:1, pp. 32–34.

Paul Mills, 'The great financial crisis: A biblical diagnosis', Cambridge Papers vol. 20, no. 1, March 2011.

Alastair Mitchell-Baker, 'Making Companies Whole: The Tricordant Approach', *FiBQ* 11:4, pp. 26–29.

Edd S. Noell, 'Bargaining, Consent and the Just Wage in the Sources of Scholastic Economic Thought', *Journal of the History of Economic Thought*, 20:4, 1998.

Joan Lockwood O'Donovan, 'Then and Now: The Schoolmen and Fair Trade', *FiBQ* 9:2, pp. 9–15.

Martin Ravaillon, 'A Comparative Perspective on Poverty Reduction in Brazil, China and India', World Bank Research Paper, 2009.

David Runton, 'Moderation in Business', *FiBQ* 8:2, pp. 21–24.

Michael Schluter, 'Is Capitalism morally bankrupt?', *Cambridge Papers* 18:3.

Geoff Shattock, 'When You See It Like This You're Never the Same: A Revolutionary Understanding of Work', *FiBQ* 12:3, pp. 3–8.

St Paul's Institute Report, *Value and Values: Perceptions of Ethics in the City Today*, November 2011.

Magne Supphellen, Sven Haugland & Ove Oklevik, 'Entrepreneurial orientation, self-efficacy, and religious attitudes in small third-world enterprises', unpublished paper.

James Walvin, 'Why were the Quakers especially good in business?', *FiBQ* 3:4, pp. 8–13.

Peter Warburton, 'Not the Rock of Ages: What should we make of the Northern Rock imbroglio?', *FiBQ* 11:3, pp. 3–6.

Lynn White Jr, 'The Historic Roots of our Ecologic Crisis', *Science* 155, 1967.

Jim Wright, "Reclaiming Business for the Kingdom of God", *FiBQ* 10:2, pp. 11–20.

N. T. Wright, "How Can The Bible Be Authoritative?", *Vox Evangelica* 21, pp. 7–32.

Ian Yearsley, "Economics without usury", *FiBQ* 11:4.

Edward W. Younkins, 'Jean-Baptiste's Law of Markets: A Fundamental, Conceptual Integration', *Le Québécois Libre*, no. 166, Feb. 2006.

NOTES

1. Faith in the economy: a power for good

1. These are figures from a World Values Survey cited by Niall Ferguson in *Civilization: The West and the Rest* (Allen Lane, 2011), p. 266.
2. *Ibid.*
3. See for example Sang-Goog Cho, 'Korean Economy: A Model Case of Miraculous Growth?', unpublished paper, 1993; Ken Eldred, *God is at Work: Transforming People and Nation through Business* (Manna Ventures, 2005), pp. 11–12, 127.
4. See Niall Ferguson, *Civilization*, pp. 284–285; Peter Heslam, 'Boss Christians: Entrepreneurs in Asia's Spiritual and Economic Awakening', *Faith in Business Quarterly (FiBQ)* 13:3, pp. 31–32.
5. Charles Hampden-Turner and Fons Trompenaars, *The Seven Cultures of Capitalism* (Little, Brown, 1995) p. 266.
6. See James Walvin, *The Quakers: Money and Morals* (John Murray, 1997) and his article 'Why were the Quakers especially good in business?', *FiBQ* 3:4, pp. 8–13.
7. Max Weber, *The Protestant Ethic and the Spirit of Capitalism* (Routledge Classics, 2001), p. 69.
8. Niall Ferguson, *Civilization*, p. 263.
9. This is argued convincingly by Simon Schama in *The Embarrassment of Riches: An Interpretation of Dutch Culture in the Golden Age* (Random House, 1987).
10. A further point made by Walvin in the article cited above.
11. Niall Ferguson, *Civilization*, p. 263.
12. Michael Novak, introduction to Amintore Fanfani, *Catholicism, Protestantism and Capitalism* (IHS Press, 2003), p. XLVIII.
13. Michael Novak, *The Spirit of Democratic Capitalism* (Madison Books, 1982). pp. 23, 239.

2. Theology in business: hindrance or help?

1. Lausanne Theology Working Group, 'A Statement on Prosperity Teaching'.

2. Craig Blomberg, *Neither Poverty nor Riches: A Biblical Theology of Possessions* (Apollos, 1999), p. 244.

3. Magne Supphellen, Sven Haugland & Ove Oklevik, 'Entrepreneurial orientation, self-efficacy, and religious attitudes in small third-world enterprises', paper given at a conference I attended in Uppsala, Sweden, in March 2011.

4. To these could be added Michael Northcott, Professor at Edinburgh University, whose *A Moral Climate: The Ethics of Global Warming* (DLT, 2007) blames industrial capitalism for the ecological crisis.

5. Timothy Gorringe, *Capital and the Kingdom: Theological Ethics and Economic Order* (SPCK, 1994), p. 159.

6. Timothy Gorringe, *Fair Shares: Ethics and the Global Economy* (Thames & Hudson, 1999), p. 102.

7. Wilf Wilde, *Crossing the River of Fire: Mark's Gospel and Global Capitalism* (Epworth, 2006), p. 13.

8. *Ibid*, p. 12.

9. *Ibid*, p. 156.

10. *Ibid*, p. 251.

11. *Ibid*, p. 12.

12. Niall Ferguson, *Civilization*, p. 146.

13. See Stephen Halliday, *The Great Stink of London: Joseph Bazalgette and the Cleansing of the Victorian Metropolis* (The History Press Ltd, 2001).

14. *Cleansing the River of Fire*, p. 12.

15. See Martin Ravaillon, 'A Comparative Perspective on Poverty Reduction in Brazil, China and India', World Bank Research Paper, 2009.

16. *Ibid*.

17. See Gustavo Gutiérrez, *A Theology of Liberation* (SCM, 1974); Leonardo Boff, *Jesus Christ Liberator* (SCM, 1978); Jon Sobrino, *Jesus the Liberator* (Orbis Books, 1993); José Porfirio Miranda, *Marx and the Bible* (SCM, 1977); Juan Luis Segundo, *The Liberation of Theology* (Orbis Books, 1976); José Miguez Bonino, *Revolutionary Theology Comes of Age* (SPCK, 1975).

18. See David Martin, *Tongues of Fire: The Explosion of Pentecostalism in Latin America* (Wiley-Blackwell, 1993).

19. Jürgen Moltmann, *A Broad Place: An Autobiography* (SCM, 2007), p. 232.

20. See Mark Greene, *The Great Divide* (LICC, 2010).
21. The Lutheran doctrine of the two kingdoms develops this understanding.
22. See archives.wittenburgdoor.com/archives/kennethlay.html – an interesting interview with Kenneth Lay.
23. Jürgen Moltmann, *A Theology of Hope*, p. 16.
24. In particular, Moltmann wrote a notable essay on 'The Right to Meaningful Work' in his book on political theology and ethics, *On Human Dignity* (Fortress, 1984).
25. Tom Wright, *Surprised by Hope* (SPCK, 2007), p. 205.
26. *Ibid*, p. 219.

3. Launched in hope: creation and entrepreneurship

1. James Jones, *Jesus and the Earth* (SPCK, 2004), p. 29.
2. Karl Barth has an interesting discussion of this boundary between creation and providential work in *Church Dogmatics* III:3 (T. & T. Clark, 1976), pp. 6–14.
3. A helpful book on this issue is Marva J. Dawn, *The Sense of the Call: A Sabbath Way of Life for Those Who Serve God, the Church, and the World* (Eerdmans, 2006), especially chapter 2.
4. John Lovatt, 'Jesus in the Workplace: Towards a Better Theology of Work'. *MC* (1992), Vol. XXXIV, No. 2, p. 14.
5. Robert Banks, *God the Worker* (Judson Press, 1994). p. v.
6. *Ibid*, pp. 276–7.
7. To be fair to Bush, the authenticity of this statement has never been confirmed!
8. Edward W. Younkins, 'Jean-Baptiste Say's Law of Markets: A Fundamental, Conceptual Integration', *Le Québécois Libre*, no. 166, Feb 2006. This can be found online at www.quebecoislibre.org/06/060212-4.htm.
9. Peter Heslam, Director of Transforming Business, also explores an understanding of God along these lines. See his *Transforming Capitalism: Entrepreneurship and the Renewal of Thrift* (Grove Books, 2010), especially chapter 3.
10. Richard Branson, *Business Stripped Bare* (Virgin Books, 2008), p. 38.
11. The early stages of this transformation were described in *The Cambridge Phenomenon: The Growth of High Technology Industry in a University Town* (Segal Quince Wickstead, 1985).

12. Five volumes have been published between 2005 and 2010, the first two under the title *The Christian Entrepreneur*.
13. Richard J. Goossen (ed.), *Entrepreneurial Leaders: Reflections on Faith at Work IV* (Trinity Western University, 2008), p. 7.
14. *Ibid*, p. 7.
15. See especially Joseph Schumpeter, *Capitalism, Socialism and Democracy* (Harper & Row, 1942), pp. 82–85.
16. Richard J. Goossen (ed.), *Entrepreneurial Leaders: Reflections on Faith at Work III* (Trinity Western University, 2007) p. 206.
17. *Ibid*, pp. 152 and 150.
18. *Ibid*, p. 168.
19. Lynn White Jr, 'The Historic Roots of our Ecologic Crisis', *Science* 155 (1967), pp. 1203–1207.
20. Ian L. McHarg, *Design with Nature* (Doubleday, 1969), p. 26.
21. See IPCC Climate Change Report 2007: www.ipcc.ch/publications_and_data/ar4/syr/en/mains1.html.
22. See 'President Bush discusses global climate change', Press Release, 11 June 2011.
23. Mark McAllister, 'An Inconvenient Truth', *FiBQ* 13:1, p. 33.
24. *Ibid*, p. 34.
25. *Ibid*.
26. See unstats.un.org/unsd/environment/air_co2_emissions.htm. These are United Nations statistics. To be fair to China, they have a much larger population and their emissions *per capita* (4.92%) are much smaller than the USA's (19.9%). The biggest polluters per capita are actually the oil-producing countries of the Middle East, with Qatar the highest – 55.43%.
27. See www.toughstuffonline.com. ToughStuff has offices in London, Madagascar and Nairobi.
28. www.eauk.org/forumforchange/culture-footprint-andrew-tanswell.cfm.

4. From hope to despair: exploitation and greed

1. Reinhold Niebuhr, *Man's Nature and his Communities* (Charles Scribner's Sons, 1965), p. 24. In fact Niebuhr was quoting an assertion he found in the *London Times Literary Supplement*.
2. www.moneymarketing.co.uk/pensions/failed-aia-bid-costs-pru-£377m/1016742.article.

3. www.morssglobalfinance.com/the-economics-of-the-global-entertainment-industry.

4. These figures come from the Stockholm Institute of Peace Research. See www.sipri.org/research/armaments/milex.

5. It should also be noted that human beings can cause terrible devastation without sophisticated weapons. The Hutus killed most of their victims in the Rwandan genocide of 1994 with machetes.

6. For Marx on alienation see in particular his *Economic and Philosophical Manuscripts* (Progress Publishers, 1959).

7. Adam Smith, *The Wealth of Nations* (Penguin, 1999), p. 12.

8. *Ibid*, p. 734.

9. See *Understanding Bonded Child Labour in Asia*, a report produced by the task force Child Workers in Asia. It can be found online at www.crin.org/docs/CWA_%20UnderstandingBondedChildLabour.pdf.

10. See 'Foxconn chief apologies for spate of suicides', www.chinadaily.com.cn/cndy/2010–05/27/content_9897265.htm; 'Undercover Report from Foxconn's Hell Factory', gizmodo.com/5542527/undercover-report-from-foxconns-hell-factory.

11. Natalie Man Se Chan, 'Making Toys in China', *FiBQ* 13:2, pp. 23–25.

12. For helpful commentaries on the crisis highlighting different aspects from three high-profile British authors, see Robert Peston, *Who Runs Britain?*, Vince Cable, *The Storm*, and Gillian Tett, *Fool's Gold*.

13. See en.wikipedia.org/wiki/United_States_public_debt. These figures come from US Government sources.

14. www.financefacts.co.uk/uk-credit-card-spending.htm.

15. www.thisismoney.co.uk/markets/article.html?in_article_id=438693.

16. Chris Patten, *What Next? Surviving the Twenty-First Century* (Allen Lane, 2008), p. 78.

17. See www.efinancialnews.com/story/2010–06–13/goldman-sachs-ethics-waiver. Citibank also has a waiver.

18. Jean Porter, 'Virtue Ethics', in Robin Gill (ed.), *The Cambridge Companion to Christian Ethics* (Cambridge University Press, 2001), p. 96.

19. David Runton, 'Moderation in Business', *FiBQ* 8:2, pp. 21–24.

20. James Allcock, 'Prudence in Business', *FiBQ* 8:2, pp. 14–20.
21. Peter Warburton, 'Not the Rock of Ages: What should we make of the Northern Rock imbroglio?', *FiBQ* 11:3, pp. 3–6.
22. Amos 1:9–10 and Joel 3:6 likewise hint of Tyre selling people as slaves.
23. David Landes, *The Wealth and Poverty of Nations* (WW Norton, 1998), p. xii.
24. Here I follow the terminology of Niall Ferguson: *Civilization: The West and the Rest.*
25. For more detail on Scandinavians' lack of corruption and their social egalitarianism, see chapters 5 and 8.
26. Lautaro Wines' Sauvignon Blanc and Merlot Reserve can be ordered from Traidcraft online – see www.traidcraftshop.co. uk/c-178–fair-trade-and-organic-wine.aspx.

5. Hope for a nation: no debt, no corruption

1. Christopher J. H. Wright, *Old Testament Ethics for the People of God* (IVP, 2004), p. 49.
2. *Ibid*, p. 51.
3. As suggested by Derek Kidner, *Proverbs* (IVP, 2008), p. 21.
4. www.sistersinbusiness.net/The%20Proverbs%2031%20Woman. htm.
5. proverbs31womanexperience.com/aboutus.aspx.
6. See Beatriz Armedavic, *The Economics of Microfinance* (MIT Press, 2005). The Grameen Bank says that 95% of their micro-lending is to women. For Christian micro-finance organisations Opportunity International and Five Talents the figures are 84% (www.opportunity.org/what-is-microfinance) and 67% (www.fivetalents.org/who-we-are/faqs#women) respectively.
7. Two influential reports advocating this change were the 1994 Latham Report, *Constructing the Team*, and the 1998 Egan Report, *Rethinking Construction*.
8. www.jewfaq.org/613.htm.
9. William J. Webb, *Slaves, Women and Homosexuals: Exploring the Hermeneutics of Cultural Analysis* (IVP, 2001), inclines to this approach.
10. *Old Testament Ethics for the People of God*, p. 63.
11. *Ibid*.

12. *Ibid.*
13. William H. Spohn, *Go and Do Likewise* (Continuum, 2000), p. 54.
14. J. W. Marshall, *Israel and the Book of the Covenant* (Atlanta, 1993), p. 148.
15. T. E. Fretheim, *Exodus* (John Knox Press, 1991), p. 247.
16. Christopher J. H. Wright, *Deuteronomy* (Hendrickson, 1996), p. 188.
17. Cyprian of Carthage, *Test.* III, 48; Gregory of Nyssa, *Hom. IV in Eccl.*
18. Lombard, *Sentences* III.37.5: II, 211.
19. Odd Langholm, *The Legacy of Scholasticism in Economic Thought* (Cambridge University Press, 1999), pp. 60–62.
20. Aquinas, *Summa Theologiae*, Qu.78, Art. 1.
21. *Ibid.*
22. *Ibid.*
23. *Op. cit,*, Qu.78, Art. 2.
24. *Ibid.*
25. Odd Langholm, *The Legacy of Scholasticism*, p. 75.
26. Martin Luther, *On Trade and Usury*, pp. 277, 281, 290, 308.
27. *Ibid.*, p. 297.
28. *Ibid*, pp. 305–306.
29. *Calvin's Ecclesiastical Advice* (Westminster/John Knox Press, 1991), pp. 139–143.
30. *Ibid*, p. 141.
31. *Ibid*, p. 142.
32. Similarly, in his commentary on Deuteronomy 23, he argues that interest is justified in cases of prolonged failure to pay a debt, or a loan taken by an already monied person in order to buy land. See Calvin, *Commentaries on the Four Last Books of Moses* (Eerdmans, 1950), pp. 125–133.
33. Norman L. Jones, 'Usury' in H. J. Hillerbrand (ed.), *Oxford Encyclopedia of the Reformation* (Oxford University Press, 1996), p. 204.
34. See Ian Yearsley, 'Economics without usury', *FiBQ* 11:4, p. 31.
35. Tarek El Diwany (ed.), *Islamic Banking and Finance* (1st Ethical Charitable Trust, 2010) is a recent book on Islamic banking and finance which covers not only personal and commercial

banking, but also wholesale finance, home purchase, investment funds, inheritance and insurance, as well as the operation of the financial markets.

36. Paul Mills, 'The great financial crisis: a biblical diagnosis', Cambridge Papers vol. 20, no. 1, March 2011, p. 3.
37. *Ibid.*
38. *Ibid*, p. 2.
39. Paul Mills, 'Finance' in Michael Schluter and John Ashcroft, *The Jubilee Manifesto* (IVP, 2005), p. 205.
40. See Brian Griffiths, 'The case for usury: biblical foundations of a modern credit economy', *FiBQ* 10:2, pp. 25–26.
41. Paul Mills, 'Finance', p. 205.
42. Paul Mills, 'The great financial crisis: a biblical diagnosis', p. 2.
43. The Relationships Foundation, which promotes the benefit of healthy relationships for social and organizational life, is a sister organization to the Jubilee Centre.
44. Niall Ferguson, *The Ascent of Money* (Penguin, 2008), p. 4.
45. John T. Noonan Jr, *Bribes* (Macmillan, 1984), p. xi.
46. *Ibid*, p. xxi.
47. George Moody-Stuart, *Grand Corruption* (WorldView Publishing, 1997), p. 42.
48. Daryl Balia, *Make Corruption History* (SPCK, 2009), pp. 115–117.
49. Hwa Yung, *Bribery and Corruption: Biblical Reflections and Case Studies for the Marketplace in Asia* (Graceworks, 2010), p. 26.
50. Bernard Adeney, *Strange Virtues* (IVP, 1995), p. 152.
51. The definition derives from US economist Joseph Senturia in an article he wrote for the *Encyclopaedia of Social Sciences* in 1931.
52. See George Moody-Stuart, *Grand Corruption*, especially pp. 58–60.
53. For example, at a consultation on *Tackling Corruption in Business* we ran at Ridley Hall in 1999; I reflect on this in Richard Higginson, *Questions of Business Life* (Authentic Media, 2002), ch. 8.
54. This seminar was organized by SAIACS, the South Asian Institute for Advanced Christian Studies, in Bangalore. It took place on 24 July 2010.
55. *Bribery and Corruption*, p. 25.
56. *Make Corruption History*, p. 147.

57. When I visited Lagos in 2005, I watched a television programme which devoted an hour to the activities of the Obisanjo government's anti-corruption agency.
58. *Make Corruption History*, pp. 58–61.

6. Hope in a son: helping the marginalized

1. Jeremiah 38; 2 Chronicles 24:20–21.
2. As is evident from the fact that he was conceived before Mary was married, the arduous journey to Bethlehem and the flight to Egypt.
3. www.qub.ac.uk/schools/SchoolofEnglish/visual-culture/painting/Christ-pre-raphaelite.html.
4. John Browne, *Beyond Business* (Phoenix, 2011), pp. 22–23.
5. *Ibid*, p. 26.
6. www.gsk.com/mission-strategy.
7. This is especially true of the Indian Dalit theologians. See www.csichurch.com/article/dalit.htm.
8. In the two versions of the Beatitudes, Jesus says 'Blessed are the poor' in Luke (6:20) and 'Blessed are the poor in spirit' in Matthew (5:3).
9. E.g. Ben Witherington III, *Jesus and Money* (SPCK, 2010), pp. 96–97; John Howard Yoder, *The Politics of Jesus* (Eerdmans, 1972), pp. 34–40, 64–77.
10. Some people question whether the Jubilee was ever put into effect, since it is scarcely mentioned in the rest of the Old Testament and its programme would seriously threaten the vested interests of the rich and powerful. However, Hillel, the influential Jewish Rabbi who lived from 65 BC to 10 AD, spoke about the Jubilee as a living institution, so there may have been periodic attempts to implement it.
11. In particular, Jesus taught a positive rather than negative approach to Sabbath observance. I say more about Mary Magdalene and Zacchaeus later in this chapter.
12. See www.tricordant.com and Alastair Mitchell-Baker, 'Making Companies Whole: The Tricordant Approach', *FiBQ* 11:4, pp. 26–29.
13. Richard Higginson, 'Can Business Be Christian? A report on a Ridley Hall Foundation conference', *FiBQ* 7:3, p. 20.

14. Brittany Smith, 'Christians Help the Poor with Renewable Energy', *The Christian Post*, 9 January 2012. See www.christianpost.com/news/christians-help.

15. The phrase 'kingdom of God' occurs eight times in parallel passages in Mark, Matthew and Luke, three times in parallel passages in Mark and Matthew, ten times in parallel passages in Matthew and Luke, twice in parallel passages in Mark and Luke, twenty-five times in Matthew only (Matthew preferring to use the phrase 'kingdom of *heaven*'), and ten times in Luke only.

16. A major theme in Richard Burridge's book on New Testament Ethics, *Imitating Jesus* (Eerdmans, 2007), is that to understand Jesus' ethics we must pay as much attention to what he did as what he said.

17. Edd S. Noell, 'Bargaining, Consent and the Just Wage in the Sources of Scholastic Economic Thought', *Journal of the History of Economic Thought*, 20:4, 1998, p. 476.

18. Richard Higginson and David Clough, *The Ethics of Executive Pay* (Grove Books, 2010), pp. 21–23.

19. John Hughes, 'Work, prayer and leisure in the Christian tradition', *Crucible*, Jan–Mar 2011, p. 10.

20. G. B. Caird, *The Gospel of St Luke* (Pelican, 1963), p. 180.

21. On the tax collector system in New Testament times see Richard Horsley, *Jesus and the Spiral of Violence* (Augsburg Fortress, 1992), pp. 212–213.

22. See Shirley K. Drew, Melanie Mills and Bob Gassway, *Dirty Work: The Social Construction of Taint* (Baylor University Press, 2007), for an interesting investigation of the experience of doing useful but low-status jobs.

23. See my analysis of the causes of the crisis in chapter 4.

24. *The Economist*, 2 May 2011, available online at www.economist.com/economist-asks/international_banking_question_4.

25. For instance, hedge fund owners Paul Marshall and Ian Wace are the co-founders of ARK (Absolute Return for Kids), which raises charitable contributions from the hedge fund industry for children who are victims of abuse, disability, illness and poverty. See www.arkonline.org and www.enotes.com/topic/Marshall_Wace.

26. I shall say more on the subject of restraint and top executive pay in chapter 7.

27. See his great diatribe against the scribes and Pharisees in Matthew 23 where he repeatedly calls them 'hypocrites' – verses 15, 17, 23, 25, 27 and 29.
28. The most striking example of this genre is Titian's *Mary Magdalene* in the Pitti Palace, Florence.
29. G. B. Caird, *The Gospel of St Luke*, p. 114.
30. *Ibid.*
31. See www.onlineschools.org/blog/stats-on-prostitution, which provides sources for these statistics.
32. Andy Matheson, *In His Image* (Authentic Media, 2009), p. 62.
33. Beacon of Hope is a similar organisation working among women in Rongai, another low-income area of Nairobi.

7. The death and resurrection of hope: integrity, sacrifice and vindication

1. Early twentieth-century Scottish theologians James Denney and P. T. Forsyth repeatedly referred to Jesus' death as the Work of Christ.
2. Geoff Shattock, 'When You See It Like This You're Never the Same: A Revolutionary Understanding of Work', *FiBQ* 12:3, p. 4.
3. These figures include the 343 firefighters and 60 police who were killed, but not the 147 people on board the two planes, nor the hijackers.
4. Douglas Kellner, '9/11, Spectacles of Terror and Media Manipulation: A Critique of Jihadist and Bush Media Politics'. This article can be found at gseis.ucla.edu/faculty/kellner/essays/911terrorspectaclemedia.pdf.
5. As indicated by Osama bin Laden's various taped broadcasts.
6. Citizens from 77 different countries died in 9/11, including many Muslims.
7. Another 1.7 million people die from occupational diseases. See www.ilo.org/global/topics/safety-and-health-at-work/lang--en/index.htm.
8. www.hse.gov.uk/statistics/fatals.htm.
9. John Browne, *Beyond Business* (Phoenix, 2011), pp. 203, 204.
10. Susan E. Squires *et al.*, *Inside Arthur Andersen* (FT Press, 2003), describes the weakening of a firm once renowned for its high standards of business ethics in the two decades before Enron.

11. Adam Smith, *The Wealth of Nations* (Penguin, 1999), p. 14.
12. www.educationalrap.com/song/maximum-utility.html.
13. www.riskmetrics.com/press/articles/20080816_smh.html.
14. Richard Wilkinson and Kate Pickett, *The Spirit Level* (Allen Lane, 2009). Although the general mental health of Sweden and Japan is better, these two countries do have quite high rates of suicide. This suggests that individuals who resist the social conformity that tends to go with egalitarianism experience severe stress.
15. For a helpful account and interesting critique of economic orthodoxy's view of human beings as rational self-interested utility seekers, see Donald E. Frey, 'The Good Samaritan as Bad Economist', www.crosscurrents.org/frey2.html.
16. C. Hoyos and M. Steen, 'Shell chief calls for pay reforms, *Financial Times*, 8 June 2009, http://goo.gl/X@dl. Van der Veer received a salary of 10.3m euros in 2008, his final year of office.
17. Lewis Smith, '"Unrepentant" Diamond set to bank £9m bonus', *The Independent*, 5 February 2011, http://search.independent. co.uk/topic/package-worth-bob-diamond. In the end Barclays awarded Diamond a £6.5m bonus.
18. Sushil Mohan, *Fair Trade Without the Froth* (IEA, 2010), p. 35.
19. www.fairtrade.org.uk/what_is_fairtrade/facts_and_figures.aspx.
20. A helpful summary of seven independent studies which have measured the impact of fair trade on producers can be found at en.wikipedia.org/wiki/Fair_trade_impact_studies.
21. See www.flo-cert.net/flo-cert/main.php for full details of FLO-CERT's fees.
22. Harriet Lamb, *Fighting the Banana Wars* (Rider & Co, 2008), chapters 2 and 5.
23. Sushil Mohan, *Fair Trade Without the Froth* (IEA, 2010), pp. 62–63.
24. Peter Frost and Sandra Robinson, 'The Toxic Handler: Organizational Hero – and Casualty', *Harvard Business Review*, July–August 1999, pp. 97–106. I am grateful to Eve Poole for directing me to this.
25. *Op. cit.*, p. 98.
26. Allan Bussard, 'Enterprise Solutions to Poverty', *FiBQ* 14:2.
27. The moment of surprise is superbly captured by Caravaggio in his painting of the Supper at Emmaus in the National Gallery, London.

28. NRSV translates *hilasmos* as 'atoning sacrifice', but propitiation is a more literal rendering.
29. John Stott reflects wisely on this in *The Cross of Christ* (IVP, 1986), pp. 167–168 and 228–230.
30. *The Cross of Christ*, pp. 233–234.
31. C. S. Lewis, *Miracles* (Fontana 1960), p. 116.
32. Michael Schluter, 'Is Capitalism morally bankrupt?', *Cambridge Papers* 18:3, p. 3.
33. www.johnlewispartnership.co.uk/about/our-founder/bbc-broadcast.html.
34. Margareta Pagano, 'Why John Lewis's Andy is streets ahead', *The Independent*, 14 March 2010. The title is a pun on the name of John Lewis's chief executive, Andy Street.
35. Joe Henley, 'Is John Lewis the best company in Britain to work for?', *The Guardian*, 14 March 2010. This comprised 15% bonuses all round in 2010.
36. Ambrose Evans-Pritchard, 'Spain's astonishing co-op takes on the world', *Daily Telegraph*, 16 February 2011.
37. David Erdal, *Beyond the Corporation: Humanity Working* (Random House, 2011), p. 208. Erdal is a director of the Baxi partnership. He played a key role in the employee buy-out of Loch Fyne Oysters, a company about which he has written a separate book, *Local Heroes*.
38. Muhammad Yunus, *Banker to the Poor* (Aurum Press, 1998), p. 5.
39. *Op. cit.*, p. 116.
40. nobelprize.org/nobel_prizes/peace/laureates/2006.
41. Opportunity International's original name was the Institute for International Development Incorporated (IIDI).
42. www.microensure.com/products-creditlife.asp.
43. fivetalents.org.uk/images/general/Sustain%20Awards_Mar2010.pdf.
44. www.fivetalents.org/get-involved/mission-trip-opportunities.
45. www.bridgefoundation.org.in/karnataka.html.
46. www.businessinsider.com/microfinance-suicides–2010–10.
47. worldnewsb4u.blogspot.com/2011/05/nobel-prize-winner-quits-bank-he.html.
48. fivetalents.org.uk/blog/?p=244.

49. As argued by Peter Heslam in 'Savings on a Passage to India: from Debt to Equity in a Subprime World', *FiBQ* 13:4, pp. 29–30.

8. A people of hope: enterprising monks and caring employers

1. See for example 1 Corinthians 1:26: 'not many of you were wise by human standards, not many were powerful, not many were of noble birth.'
2. See also chapters 1 and 5 which contain other important historical examples.
3. Cicero, *De Officiis*, 1:42, p. 150.
4. Eusebius, *Demonstration of the Gospel* 1.8.
5. St Augustine, Sermon 169, paragraph 17. See also *City of God*, XIX, 19.
6. Along with many other theologians, Origen being the first in *Ioan*, Fragment 80: 'Mary is the symbol of the contemplative life, Martha of the active.' In *Summa Theologiae* Qu. 182 Art. 1, Aquinas gives nine reasons, mostly based on this story, why the contemplative life is 'more excellent' than the active.
7. For more information see www.mmmongolia.com/. Ridley Hall is a mission partner of Mary and Martha Mongolia.
8. Kit Dollard, Anthony Marett-Crosby and Abbot Timothy Wright, *Doing Business with Benedict* (Continuum, 2002), p. 10.
9. *Rule of St Benedict*, 57.
10. *Op. cit.*, 31. Dollard, Marett-Crosby and Wright, p. 97, describe Benedict's vision for the Cellarer as 'one of the most carefully crafted and poised chapters in the whole text.'
11. Alain Erlande-Brandenburg, *The Cathedral Builders of the Middle Ages* (Thames & Hudson, 1993), p. 101.
12. Jean Gimpel, *The Medieval Machine: The Industrial Revolution of the Middle Ages* (Rinehart and Winston, 1976), p. 67.
13. Joan Lockwood O'Donovan, 'Then and Now: The Schoolmen and Fair Trade', *FiBQ* 9:2, p. 11.
14. *Ibid.*, p. 13.
15. For an account of Olivi's views see Odd Langholm, *Economics in the Medieval Schools* (EJ Brill, 1992), pp. 360–365. Martin Luther, who resembled the schoolmen in his views on the just price, has

a similar list in 'On Trade and Usury', *Luther's Works,* Vol. 45 (Fortress, 1962).

16. For Duns Scotus' views see Langholm, *Economics in the Medieval Schools*, pp. 410–411.
17. Robert Southey, *Life of Wesley* II (Hutchinson, 1900), p. 308.
18. Thomas Jackson (ed.), *Wesley's Sermons*, no.50. The sermon has been published as Appendix 2 in Ben Witherington III, *Jesus & Money* (SPCK, 2010), pp. 171–183. Subsequent references are to this version.
19. *Ibid*, pp. 177–178.
20. *Ibid*, p. 178.
21. *Ibid*, p. 179.
22. *Ibid*, p. 181.
23. *Ibid*, p. 182.
24. Ian Bradley, *Enlightened Entrepreneurs* (Lion Hudson, 2007), p. 12.
25. *Ibid*, p. 14.
26. *Ibid*, p. 37.
27. *Ibid*, p. 41.
28. The saying is often attributed to Prime Minister Harold Wilson, who certainly repeated it, but was first made by Labour Party General Secretary Morgan Phillips.
29. Some of this legislation was introduced by the Liberal Government of 1906–14, but pressure from the emerging Labour Party played its part.
30. David H. Jensen, *Responsive Labor* (Westminster/John Knox Press, 2006), p. 80.
31. Words from Eucharistic Prayer D in Church of England, *Common Worship* (Church House Publishing, 2000), p. 195.
32. David H. Jensen, Fed and Hungry at Christ's Table: Daily Work and the Abundance of Eucharist', *FiBQ* 11:1, p. 7.
33. *Common Worship*, p. 182.

9. Hope for the future: signs of the kingdom

1. This is often associated with a 'rapture' theology, popularized by best-selling books such as Hal Lindsey's *The Late Great Plane Earth* and Tim LaHaye's *Left Behind* series.
2. Miroslav Volf, *Work in the Spirit* (Oxford University Press, 1991), p. 89.

3. *Ibid*, p. 91.
4. This occurred on 16–17 July 2011.
5. John Lovatt, my colleague in editing *Faith in Business Quarterly*, argues this strongly in 'All Things', *FiBQ* 13:2, pp. 3–11.
6. Michael Wilcock, *I Saw Heaven Opened: The Message of Revelation* (IVP, 1975), p. 211.
7. See page XXX.
8. Richard Mouw, *When the Kings Come Marching In: Isaiah and the New Jerusalem* (Eerdmans, 1983), p. 28.
9. *Ibid.*, p. 39.
10. John Donne, *Meditation XVII*.
11. Jim Wright, 'Reclaiming Business for the Kingdom of God', *FiBQ* 10:2, p. 14. This article was based on the talk he gave at the 2006 Faith in Business conference on *Past, Present and Future: Christian Faith and Business Practice*.
12. *Op. cit.*, p. 11.
13. See quotation cited on page XXX.
14. James Jones, *Jesus and the Earth*, p. 60. Another theologian who adopts this language and takes a transformationist approach is Darrell Cosden. See his *The Heavenly Good of Earthly Work* (Paternoster, 2006).
15. For more information on Broetje Orchards, see Kenman L. Wong and Scott B. Rae, *Business for the Common Good* (IVP, 2011), pp. 251–253.
16. Miroslav Volf, *Work in the Spirit*, p. 100.

10. Faith, hope and love: an alternative vision for business

1. Cited by Niall Ferguson in *Empire: How Britain Made the Modern World* (Penguin, 2003), p. 154.
2. Luigi Guiso, Paola Sapienza and Luigi Zingales, *People's Opium? Religion and Economic Attitudes*, NBER Working Paper 9237. This can be found at www.kellogg.northwestern.edu/faculty/sapienza/htm/religion.pdf.
3. *Ibid*, pp. 5–7.
4. Francis Fukuyama, *Trust: The Social Virtues and the Creation of Prosperity* (Penguin, 1995), p. 142.

5. I am here developing ideas helpfully outlined by N. T. Wright, "How Can The Bible Be Authoritative?", *Vox Evangelica* 21, pp. 7–32, and Samuel Wells, *Improvisation: The Drama of Christian Ethics* (SPCK, 2004), ch. 3. But I have more separate acts in the drama than they do in theirs.

6. See H. Richard Niebuhr, *Christ and Culture* (Harper & Row, 1951). Eve Poole helpfully summarizes Niebuhr's argument in *The Church on Capitalism: Theology and the Market* (Palgrave Macmillan, 2010), pp. 94–100.

7. Kenman L. Wong & Scott B. Rae, *Business for the Common Good: A Christian Vision for the Marketplace* (IVP Academic, 2011), p. 284.

8. www.tbnetwork.org; www.transformingbusiness.net.

9. www.ica.coop/coop/statistics.html.

10. See John Browne, *Beyond Business* (Phoenix, 2011), pp. 113–117.

11. www.jnj.com/connect/about-jnj/jnj-credo.

12. This story is told by Jim Wright in his article 'Reclaiming Business for the Kingdom of God', *FiBQ* 10:2, pp. 19–20. I have put the story into the first person.

discover more great Christian books
at www.ivpbooks.com

Full details of all the books from Inter-Varsity Press – including
reader reviews, author information, videos and free downloads –
are available on our website at **www.ivpbooks.com**.

IVP publishes a wide range of books on various subjects including:

Biography

Christian Living

Bible Studies

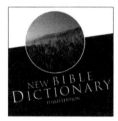

Reference

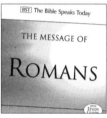

Commentaries

Theology

On the website you can also sign up for regular email newsletters,
tell others what you think about books you have read by posting
reviews, and locate your nearest Christian bookshop using the
Find a Store feature.

IVP publishes Christian books that are **true to the Bible**
and that **communicate the gospel, develop discipleship**
and **strengthen the church** for its mission in the world.